Jerusalem Creek

Jerusalem Creek

Journeys into Driftless Country

Ted Leeson

THE LYONS PRESS

GUILFORD, CONNECTICUT

An Imprint of The Globe Pequot Press

The Lyons Press is an imprint of The Globe Pequot Press.

Printed in the United States of America

2 4 6 8 10 9 7 5 3 1

Design by Compset, Inc.

The Library of Congress Cataloging-in-Publication Data is available on file.

To B. and G., L. and H.

Contents

~~~~~~~~~

Acknowledgments

Sometimes a book, impatient to be written, shows up one day on your doorstep uninvited, just stopping by for old time's sake. It greets you like a long-lost friend, makes cheerful small talk on the porch, slugs you in the shoulder and says you're looking good, buddy boy, but will not go away. And at last, because you were brought up to be polite, you ask it inside, full of misgivings and doubts but also that distant sense of obligation you might feel for a person with whom you shared a brief, but intense, association—an old college roommate who flunked out and nearly took you with him, or someone you once did time with. You try to be pleasant, but you keep looking at the clock, until it becomes clear that your guest has no intention of leaving. It likes your house and means to stay. It takes to staying up till all hours, drinking your beer, and sleeping on the sofa; it borrows the car without permission and steals your spare change. By the time you consider phoning the police, it has been there so long you fear there might be legal repercussions.

First and deepest thanks to my wife, Elizabeth Campbell, who willingly accommodated this visitor and humored its moods and, when the time came, quite materially assisted in its removal. Named or not, she is on every page.

I am indebted as well to Tracy Daugherty for his careful reading of the manuscript and judicious suggestions. Thanks to a trio of Jims: to Jim Babb for sage advice and an even keel; to Jim Butler for helping me clear the decks; to Jim Schollmeyer for keeping my shoulder to the wheel, then periodically checking for broken bones. I am grateful, as always, to Nick Lyons for counsel, support, and a keen eye; to Steve Born, of the University of Wisconsin at Madison, for patiently fielding questions about the driftless area; to Trevor Walker, whose letters on spring-creek hydrology were both illuminating and elegant; to Robert Gorman for all manner of generosity; and to Brian Barker for the soundtrack.

Thanks, finally, to Cletus, Paul, Edwina, Mick, and Rip, friends by any name.

I had never known before how short life really was, and into how small a space the mind could put it.

—Charles Dickens, *Bleak House*

Introduction
Small Thrills

～～～～～～

Shortly before I turned twenty, I stumbled into one of those periodic, single-author reading jags that I suspect are familiar to almost anyone with an appetite for books. For reasons I can no longer reconstruct, the writer in this instance was Ernest Hemingway, and I began systematically making my way through the complete works at a time when reading Hemingway had not yet become an act of patriarchal hegemony, nor enjoying him a mark of political and literary Philistinism. Book binges of this sort invariably prove a mixed experience; some of the work appeals and much does not, a circumstance for which reader and writer usually bear about equal responsibility. As unsophisticated readers will, I liked best what I found most familiar, even though it should be the other way around, and so was predictably drawn to the passages and stories about trout fishing, which lay closer to home and heart than the battlefields of Europe and bullrings of Spain.

I eventually found my way to the short story "Now I Lay Me," in which the narrator, badly wounded, is lying in a hospital in Milan. At night, he does not allow himself to fall asleep, certain that if he closes his eyes and lets go of consciousness, his soul will leave his body. To remain awake and stave off death, or at least the fear of it, he thinks back to a trout river in his boyhood and begins fishing it in his mind, deliberately and meticulously recalling each particular pool and bend, every log in the water, each shallow and riffle, until he has walked the entire stream. When he finishes, he begins again, fishing the water over and over, holding on to life (or so it seems to him) by an act of imagination, by summoning into being the presence of something that has mattered.

It is, in part, a story about the nature of memory, about the sustaining power of the stories we create from it and tell to ourselves, and it left me utterly astonished. For I had, over the previous few years, been doing exactly the same thing as Hemingway's narrator and for reasons that seemed at the time at least distantly similar. Though I'd so far avoided confinement in an Italian military hospital, I was a fairly typical American teenager—that is, a temporary sociopath, prey to the familiar bouts of troubled uncertainty, shapeless dread, objectless longing, and free-floating despair that afflict the no longer adolescent but not yet adult. And in my case, all of it was undoubtedly made worse by a certain sympathy for that brand of romantic self-dramatization that is eternally fashionable among the young. When the dark times descended, I would close my eyes and fish in my mind, over and over again, a particular spring creek in the southwestern corner of Wisconsin.

That trout stream was to me at the time one of the loveliest places on earth, a small creek that threaded its way down a secluded little valley. In my imagination, I walked and waded its various sections, in no order other than the sequence in which I had come to know them. But in the end I covered the entire length, from the lowest reaches, where the water was too warm for anything but the rumors of enormous brown trout with a taste for field mice and ducklings, to the upper end, where the creek first became too small to fish, then a trickle too small for trout. The distance, at best, was perhaps a mile and a half. I could bring to mind each meandering curve where the current ran cool and dark inside a shaded bend, every short shallow run over broken limestone rubble, each place where the stream broadened and pooled. I knew all the runs with steep earthen banks overgrown in the succulent stems of jewelweed, with their midsummer profusion of orchidlike blooms that glowed the color of candle flame. Here, on a warm afternoon, you could watch the ruby-throated hummingbirds come and go, not so much flying as suddenly dissolving and rematerializing somewhere else in a staccato so rapid that the sound of thrumming wings was the only assurance that you'd seen something at all. Wild mint grew in patches along the bank, a deep-green leaf with a deep-green smell, a spiciness that could not possibly be animal or mineral in origin. Where the creek wound through a pasture, half a dozen dairy cows cropped the grass as close as a golf green, and in the heat of the day, they would lounge in the shade of an oak grove, their enormous, taut udders resting on the ground. Under these same trees, out of the sun, tangles of bittersweet nightshade thrived all season long in the damp margin of the stream, some of the vinelike stems ripe with scarlet berries, others just blooming, rich purple petals with stamens the color of egg yolk. In the still backwaters, aquatic

Ranunculus sank roots in the silty streambed, growing gradually upward into a dense tangle of vegetation on the surface, and finally sending up short straight stems above the water, each topped with a single white flower like a strawberry blossom. Here and there, a spring bubbled almost imperceptibly at the water's edge, visible first as a saucer of fine, pale gravel, then as a small upwelling in which grains of sand continually rose and fell on tiny pillows of water. Groundwater seeped into meadow swales and trickled to the creek in courses marked by lush bands of watercress. I even went Hemingway one better: for some years, I could call to mind nearly every trout I'd ever caught in the stream, admittedly a number small enough to place little strain on the memory. If I didn't know this spring creek inch by inch, I was certain I knew it foot by foot, and even now, almost thirty-five years since the first time I fished it and nearly ten since the last, the place still lives in my mind with a photographic vividness.

At night, in the space behind my eyelids, I fished that spring creek hundreds of times—far more than I ever fished the real thing—and in the turmoils, both real and self-inflicted, of life at the threshold of adulthood, I found a kind of calm restored by these meticulous and crisply detailed evocations. They went beyond the escapist fantasy of simple daydreaming, however—an indulgence I knew well enough to tell the difference—and beyond the refuge of a pleasant reverie or the consoling recollections of untroubled days. Summoning those images to mind, in fact, felt less like going back and recalling the past than it did transporting those images into the present and reconstructing the place, detail by detail, to make it real then and there. It possessed the texture of actual perception, the immediacy of lived experience, and differed from mere reverie in the way that déjà vu differs from memory. I didn't set about to remember a particular morning or afternoon spent on that stream, or to envision the next trip and plan how and where I would fish; I was trying to bring the place itself into being. And while it possessed a certain meditative character, it wasn't meditation, which, at least from what I have read about it, strives first for an emptying of consciousness; I was trying to fill mine up with images of sufficient volume to displace whatever was troubling me.

Just why this place should have had so powerful an effect upon me and impress itself so durably on a brain with proven resistance to more pressing information—irregular German verbs and the equations of modern physics—was a question I would not get around to addressing for quite a while, long after I'd left the Midwest for good. To put a name to the things that haunt us is a ticklish business, often best undertaken from a distance. At the time, I felt only some unspecifiable rapport with a sliver of landscape that, by the ordinary measures of extraordinary places, was most unremarkable. It lacked the drama of sublime geographies, their sweep and vastness, their capacity to overwhelm. It was neither distant nor exotic, had no grizzly bears or waterfalls, snowy peaks or parrots. It hadn't remotely resembled wilderness for better than two centuries. Rounding the blacktop curves that descend the hillside, you might be drawn to look for a moment as the valley and creek and bottomland opened into view, would probably think it rather pretty, then go back to fiddling with the radio.

But to my eyes, it was completely captivating, although its beauties were of a quiet sort, its charms modest and proportioned to the pace of a slow walk or, better yet, of sitting still. It was not a landscape that you hiked up, or climbed down into, or stood looking out upon; it was one that you slipped inside of. The nuances of color and contour, the slope of dark hills and curve of bright water, the drape of trees and grasses, meadows laced with birdsong and wingbeats, the air electric with the hum and rattle of insects, the humid smell of decay and growth, the texture of exuberant fertility—all of these made it a profoundly wonderful place. That trout lived there made it perfect. I was drawn to the countless particulars of the landscape, the hints of its hidden life and, as I came to realize later, drawn to something else as well, a quality that inhered in its details, was in fact created by them, but that also subsumed them—something I can describe no more precisely than as the scale on which the place made itself felt.

Neither long nor wide to begin with, the stream and the valley that cradled it were made smaller still by the fact that I first ventured there as a fisherman and so approached it in a fisherman's way, not with an eye toward the whole at once but to one promising spot at a time. An angler learns the water piecemeal, beginning in each new spot by shrinking even the largest river to the compass of a cast, measuring out the boundaries of a space that, for a time, exists to the exclusion of all others. What lies inside so fully captures your attention and engages the senses that whatever takes place outside those borders is beyond awareness. This contraction of the world, concentrating it to a local and immediately present space, sometimes furthers the catching of fish, but beyond that it is, simply in and of itself, one of the best parts of fishing.

A good fisherman can create such spaces anywhere, but in certain fortunate places the landscape defines its own enclosures, draws natural boundaries in near perfect accord with your own inclinations. My spring creek, a continuous meander worn deeply into the soft valley soil, a succession of arcs and oxbows and contours etched by the current, a figure of sheer curvature, sculpts an extraordinary variety of these small spaces. If you stand at the water's edge, steep banks topped with tall grasses or trees rise higher than your head, like miniature canyons; a short way upstream, the water curls around a bend and into view, flows briefly past you, then turns another bend just downstream and disappears. Each arc in the stream becomes a world complete, a parenthetical space that gives you the distinct feeling of being inside something.

In a few short seasons of fishing there, I came to know each spot on the stream as a discrete and separate place, becoming familiar with the minute topographies of its streambed and current, the names of the plants along the bank, the creatures attracted to leaves, berries, and seed pods. Some spots fished better than others, as is always the case, but I had no real favorites. Each was a lovely composition of artful accident, intricate and precise as a miniature painting. To learn them brought a wonderful kind of knowledge, but it was the scale of these small worlds, so closely proportioned to the reach of human senses, so effortlessly inhabiting the imagination, that made them knowable at all. Later, I came to see that this sense of scale, and what it made possible, was the taproot of my attachment to the place.

∿∿∿∿∿∿∿

Though I rarely venture into French philosophy, and never without rubber boots and a cattle prod, Gaston Bachelard does have much to say about this predilection for the small scale, which he calls "the love of miniature." He attributes to this affinity a kind of rejuvenating power; to become absorbed in the small scale invests the world with the freshness of hidden things. I find it interesting, perhaps inevitable, that Bachelard should have begun his distinguished career as a philosopher of science. He possesses a scientist's eye, alert to intricacies, attuned to detail, and he explains the love of miniature not only as it appears in literature and the visual arts but in botany as well. The botanist with a hand lens, he says, studies the tiny structures of a flower and delights not only in their detail but in their scale, in the world they create and its proportion to what lies beyond the blossom. Such an observer continually encounters the fresh and undiscovered, and in perceiving them he recovers "the enlarging gaze of a child." His vision is "youth recaptured."

To call this kind of vision "youthful," I think, goes beyond a simple metaphor describing the innocent, impressionable eye confronting novelty. For the love of miniature seems a nearly universal feature of childhood. Children seek out worlds that are commensurate with their own somewhat miniature selves. Though I am not a parent, a fact for which the world has yet to show proper gratitude, I've watched other people's children explore an unfamiliar room and invariably gravitate with a perfect and automatic accuracy to whatever is small, readily graspable, and usually breakable, drawn less by the specific object than the magnificent temptation of its size. This same impulse shows itself in the love of dolls; of diminutive tea sets; of toys with small, easily swallowed parts; of tiny boxes with fitted lids that house tinier treasures still. It is in a child's love of secrets, that admission into a small world of knowing. It is the allure of the treehouse, of the damp dirt-floored space beneath a porch, of a cardboard box big enough to crawl into and pretend is something else. It is the delight in pretending itself, for pretending is a form of storytelling, and a story is but another kind of miniature. And what is not already small is made so as children set up little households and schoolrooms modeled after those of the adult world. Then, of course, within the boundaries of these scaled-down replicas, they proceed without pause to wield power over one another—a less flattering imitation of adulthood but also a way of addressing the basic human need for making one's existence felt, for somehow registering on the seismic instruments of life. It may well be one reason that children construct such worlds in the first place.

Most often, I think, the love of miniature fades with age. Children literally grow out of it; they successively appropriate worlds of larger dimension and scope as they become older, shedding the confinements of a too small life like the molt of an ill-fitting skin. But for some, the imaginative appeal of the small scale never loses its power. It is not a stage you go through, some temporary fact of psychological life; rather, like left-handedness or perfect pitch, it is a part of your makeup hard-wired from birth that will find a way to express itself with or without you. To such temperaments, the world engages most fully through the local and particular, and the lightest weights leave the deepest imprints. The anatomy of a single feather is more fascinating than the bird, and a bird a greater marvel than the flock. Small architectures—a honeycomb or caddisfly case, a milkweed pod or the web of an orb weaver, the fingerprint of a shell fossilized in limestone—are worth all the cathedrals of France. Like any angler, I hope to catch large trout, but I would much rather look at a small one; its coloration and markings are more precisely defined, deeper and purer. This is not an illusion. The color of a trout is carried less in its skin than its scales; a smaller fish has smaller scales, tinier pixels with richer definition and a higher resolution. There is a certain kind of perfection in the miniature, and behind it lies the pleasure of simply seeing close up, of experiencing the kind of proximity that the small scale not only requires but makes possible at all.

Out of this experience of proximity, of seeing and being close up, grows the love of small-scale spaces, those temporary dwelling places lit with immediacy and vividness. The oxbow pool of spring creek screened by tall grass, the yellow globe of low light in a darkened room or the halo of a campfire in the night, the cast of black shade beneath a white oak, the hull of a canoe on a lake or driftboat on a river, the circle of a lover's arms, a one-room cabin in Maine, a ring of chairs on a wooden porch up in the Montana benchlands—these to me are the small, near spaces into which, for a brief time, an immensity of living is somehow compressed. And not all such spaces are physical ones. Some take shape in the imagination, created by the elegant enclosure of a lyric poem, or the fragile lines of a sumi painting, or the sweaty interiority of the bluesman's voice, or the diameter of community. And still other places are empty ones—a void opened by words spoken or the hollow worn by words unsaid, a hole in the heart left by one now gone, a vacancy of grief that rises from the pit of you and presses the air from your lungs. For not all small spaces are happy ones. They are just keenly felt because in the end you have no choice.

In the years before we were married, my wife, who is more closely attentive to the small scale than anyone I've known, showed me another of its dimensions and taught me to appreciate enclosures in time, an awareness that she described as a "sense of occasion." It has nothing to do with celebrating the familiar milestones of life, the birthdays or anniversaries or holidays, nothing so noteworthy as to invite public acknowledgment. Rather, it is the ritual recognition of certain small moments, stillnesses in the current of living where significance settles—some little victory won from the world, a hard time weathered, the first grosbeak of spring or the last slant of autumn sun, a safe return. Such moments are ceremonially observed by deliberately inhabiting them, marking the passing of time by suspending it for a while.

This affinity for the small scale may, as Bachelard observes, involve its childlike perspective, but it is not always child's play as you come to understand that it lies much closer to the heart. Though the experience of the small scale is at first an act of discovery, in time it becomes an act of creation as you recognize that the sense of scale resides in boundaries and in how close together they are, and that boundaries can be deliberately drawn. The scale becomes small because we choose to frame it that way, marking the imaginary lines that define the outermost limits of our regard, and laying a kind of claim to what lies inside. This drawing of borders is a way of domesticating spaces and times, of making them knowable by making them proximate. It is, in short, a way of establishing, or at least searching for, a kind of intimacy with and within them.

Looking back now, I believe that what appealed to me so powerfully in the small spring creek and the landscape it had formed was the possibility they held out for a sort of intimacy, though at the time I wouldn't—couldn't—have described it to myself like this. Back then, it was just the one place above all others that I dearly and somewhat inexplicably loved to be, even when I wasn't fishing—a circumstance, I concede, that was rare. And while it may seem odd, I think too that the sense of intimate scale first drew me to fly fishing at about this same time; that the few trout I caught on flies were also small in scale didn't trouble me in the least. Even from the outset, I understood that fly fishing was a matter of borders, of self-imposed limitation, of bargains struck with no one but yourself to establish the terms on which you meet a river. Boundaries, of course, lie wherever you draw them, and there is no end to the disputes. The dry-fly purist looks at the split-shot artist and sees a knave, who stares back at him and beholds a fool. But we fix the matter in a way that pleases us most, and from there on out follow the logic of its demands. If you wish to catch trout by imitating the appearance and behavior of small lives—the fundamental enterprise of fly fishing—you must think in proportion to the place.

To fashion borders like this, to enclose within the brackets of consciousness certain spaces, or times, or even the behavior on a trout stream that is called "fly fishing" is, I think, what makes intimacy possible. And though boundaries necessarily exclude, this exclusion brings with it a clarifying power. What lies within the borders is enlarged because the whole sense of proportion changes. As you adjust to a scaled-down world, undifferentiated impressions separate into distinct details; small things seem larger; what at first passed without notice becomes perceptible. Sounds are amplified, the eyes see more acutely, the imagination leaps with greater ease because the distances are shorter. There is a magnifying power to localness that conducts us inward to the animate heart of things. Within the borders of a poem, one line emerges, and the line converges on a single word, electric with reverberations that course back through the poem like nerve endings. Deep inside a solo, Coltrane blows a long, reedy quaver that catches in your throat like a knucklebone, two centuries of pain, rage, and solace distilled to a single tone. Everything in a spring creek, the constancy of temperature and flow, the chemistry of the water, the meandering shape, the streambed geology, terrestrial and aquatic plants, zooplankton, insects, crustaceans, predators and prey—all condense to one trout holding in a shady bend.

This is not mysticism. It is the nature of our faculties to wander, to rove and search, to sniff and sample the world. And within the borders of the small scale, this restlessness turns inward, trading wider range for greater discrimination and a higher resolving power. The closer you look, the more you see, and seeing more draws you in to look closer still, to uncover not only hidden anatomies but the lines of force that hold them together in the small ecologies of a poem or piece of music, a circle of friends or a moment of time, a bend in a trout stream. Intricacies converge to reveal simplicity, which in turn unfolds into new intricacy; complexities coalesce into unities that give birth to new complexity, in a continual, spiraling, inward alternation that is the pulse of science and art alike. The concentrations of the small scale amplify our own concentration, and awareness itself, Bachelard says, becomes a magnifying glass that enlarges whatever it dwells upon.

This is the secret, paradoxical thrill of the small scale—that the more time you spend there, the less small it becomes. Its limits are a kind of liberation; worlds unfold and expand, and the distances between them are easily bridged by the imagination. In the end, we can shrink to enlarge—our perceptions, our understanding, our sympathies—and the love of the small scale, though it always remains particular, ceases to be specific. Because I cherish one spring creek that I know intimately, I value dozens of streams that I have never seen or fished; I've written words and checks on their behalf all in the belief that the love of place reaches beyond the place itself. To see beauty or repose in the curve of a creek, discover wisdom in a handful of words, or trace grief on a single face makes us receptive to these things in other places and other times. And this belief, that the significance of the local transcends locality, is what redeems the love of the small scale from mere provincialism and egocentricity.

All that lies behind this redemption is the simple trust that boundaries can be mindfully drawn, that our actions within them are consequential, that what they surround has value, and that their loss would impoverish life. But this is just a belief and like all beliefs may be only a self-deception, a story we invent for ourselves. It is entirely possible that deliberate reductions in scale are only a form of surrender, that all thrills are small because the world holds no large ones. It is possible, too, that the borders we draw enclose only ourselves, a form of self-protection, a mark of spiritual timidity.

Or worse, the small scale may enclose nothing significant at all, and our actions within it have no consequence. Certainly we have decimated hundreds of small worlds without apparent repercussion to ourselves. The eastern mountain lion, the white pine forests of the upper Midwest, the plains bison, the Redfish Lake sockeye, the Modocs—all are gone, or effectively so. The ground-zero deserts of the Southwest have been contaminated beyond imagination, Prince William Sound sacrificed as unavoidable collateral damage, the sacred space of the Black Hills chiseled to chauvinistic tourist graffiti. And yet we have not merely survived but flourished. Although the world appears a diminished place, it is by no means clear, at least yet, that the loss we sense goes any meaningful distance beyond the sentimental.

Perhaps all we can urge in the face of loss is a potentially groundless conviction that the small scale is consequential, a belief that things somehow matter—that, and the stories we create about those things, the way we fish them in our minds. Held up against an abundant evidence to the contrary, these can seem at times thin and intermittent consolations. Yet certain small pieces of the world do penetrate the heart, sometimes filling it and sometimes drawing blood, but a sign of life in either case. And if, in the end, all that can be said is that you feel them to be true, that is enough, at least in my book.

1

Springs Eternal

≈≈≈≈≈≈≈≈

From a perennial spring that runs away and is unclouded pour

three measures of water, and the fourth of wine.

—Hesiod, *Works and Days*

If you add it all up—the oceans, lakes, ponds, rivers, and creeks—the world contains about 318 million cubic miles of liquid water. Another 10 million cubic miles are locked in ice caps, trapped in aquifers and soil moisture, and drifting as vapor in the atmosphere. Of the liquid surface water, only about .0001 percent—one-millionth of it—flows in stream channels at any given time. From here, calculating the amount of moving water that furnishes habitat for trout is a dicey business at best. Gary Borger has estimated that less than one-millionth of 1 percent of the world's river water flows in trout streams. Under no authority greater than my willingness to hazard a guess, I would venture that perhaps no more than one-thousandth of this trout water exists in spring creeks. I could be off by several orders of magnitude here, but it would scarcely matter. Randomly dip a cup of water from anywhere on the surface of the earth, and the chances that it comes from a spring creek containing trout are inconceivably remote. A mathematician, in fact, would simply characterize it as a "non-zero probability"—an expression denoting a likelihood so tiny that you wouldn't even call it possible, like flipping a coin that lands on its edge. The most you might say is that it is not, theoretically speaking, a strict and literal impossibility. For all practical purposes, there is no such thing. It shouldn't exist, but that it does makes a spring-creek trout stream the rarest and smallest of small thrills.

Every point of view eventually generates its own vocabulary, and "spring creek" is a fisherman's word. You can search hydrology books and scarcely find it mentioned, and never with any technical rigor. In the larger view, the term vastly oversimplifies the complicated fact of moving water by confining it to a point of origin, which, even then, is not strictly accurate. But fishermen attend to a more local scale and aren't bothered much by this imprecision. We know what we mean, more or less, and in an angler's classification of moving water, the first and most significant division is drawn not between large streams and small ones, or eastern and western waters, but between freestone rivers and spring creeks. Like all amateur taxonomies, this one won't stand up to much formal scrutiny, but there is a rough logic to it.

Rivers are, among many other things, an interface between two great natural cycles. The hydrologic cycle is the more visible and familiar one. Water falls to earth as rain or snow. Some of this precipitation evaporates directly back

into the atmosphere; some is taken up by plants and then ex-
haled as water vapor in the process of photosynthesis. But
some water is captured by the uppermost layer of soil, where
it is temporarily held in surface storage. It may return to
stream channels as overland flow or filter farther downward
into a layer of soil and rock called the "vadose," wetting but
not saturating this underground zone. Part of the water may
leach out of this zone into streambeds, but some of it filters
still farther down, finally stopping when it reaches a layer of
impermeable rock. Water builds up on top of this barrier, occupying the tiny spaces between small particles of earth, or
filling the voids in a porous rock like sandstone, or collecting
in the cracks and fissures and seams of harder rock. With no
place to go, additional moisture percolating downward fills
all the available space, creating a "saturated zone"; the water
held there is true groundwater, and its uppermost surface defines the water table. It may be stored in an aquifer like this
for millennia, or it may find its way to the surface in seeps or
springs or upwellings, adding its volume to a stream, and
eventually flowing to the ocean. Water evaporates from the
surface of the ocean to fall as rain or snow in some other time
and place. The engine driving this cycle is the sun, through
heat that evaporates water and energy for plant growth.

Although we think of a river as primarily water, the geologic material of the bed is just as much a part of it, and perhaps more. The rock endures, at least for a time, but the
water is simply passing through. As hydrologists speak of the
water cycle, geologists speak of the rock cycle, a mechanism
that is less familiar and conspicuous because it occurs more
slowly and often out of sight. The crust of the earth does not
form a rigid, seamless shell; rather, it is fractured into ten or
twelve platelike pieces that float on the mantle of the planet.
They are in constant motion relative to one another, and this
mobility ultimately accounts for the birth of mountains.

When two plates collide at the edge, one of them may yield, rumpling upward into mountains like the hood of a car in a head-on wreck; the Himalayas were formed like this. When a tectonic plate on the sea floor runs up against the edge of a continent, mountains may be formed in a couple of ways. The heavier oceanic plate curls downward and slides beneath the lighter continental crust. It is not a smooth passing. Layers of sea floor are scraped off by the edge of the continent and pushed upward and inland; the Coast Ranges of the Pacific Northwest are of this type. The remaining layers of sea floor slip farther downward, where heat inside the earth, an interior sun that powers the cycle, liquefies the rock and periodically forces it back upward in the most dramatic enactment of the cycle—volcanic eruptions. The Cascade Mountains, a hundred miles east of the Pacific Coast, originated this way. Rain and snowmelt then erode the high ground. Rills and creeks carry away fine sediments; stronger currents bump and roll larger rocks over the riverbed, each click of stone on stone chipping off tiny particles, turning the mountains into pebbles and sand that wash downstream. Rock, like water, eventually makes its way back to the sea, the great reservoir of both cycles. Were the rock cycle to cease and mountain building come to an end, erosional forces would eventually smooth and flatten the earth's crust. Without high ground, there could be no rivers, and most of the world would be awash in a shallow sea.

Part rock and part water, rivers are an expression of both, a point of contact between two great revolving wheels that touch at the surface of the earth and briefly run downhill. And that hill is generally a steep one when fishermen speak of freestone streams. Waters of this type originate in high-gradient terrain, often land with enough pitch and elevation to bring the word "mountain" into at least local usage. The topography produces a tumbling, turbulent watercourse, a rocky channel with chutes and plunge pools, bouldered glides, angular rock-faced bends, cobblestone riffles, and quiet sandy backwaters. Because of the sharp rise of the surrounding land, such streams respond quickly to rain or melting snow that runs over or beneath the leaf litter and forest duff; in a heavy shower, water levels may rise dramatically in a few hours. In the absence of precipitation, freestone streams rely primarily on water that migrates downhill and laterally through the upper, unsaturated zones of soil. On well-drained, forested land—typical of mountains in trout country—this subsurface flow is the major pathway for water entering the stream. Since the geologic material is not tightly compacted, water moves through it with relative ease, and the mechanism of storage is somewhat temporary. While a drop of rain may take months or more to make its way from the soil surface to the stream, it still travels quickly compared to the much slower transmission of water through an aquifer.

In the summer, when rain is intermittent, evaporation rates are high, and the consumption of water by plants reaches a seasonal maximum, this water supply is gradually depleted; stream recharge slows, and water levels drop. A mountain stream may be fed by true groundwater as well, but the rock from which mountains are built typically lacks the porous structure necessary for water storage and makes a poor aquifer, and the contribution to the stream from seeps and springs is ordinarily small. By late summer, stream flows reach their annual low; the water warms, and the amount of dissolved oxygen declines. As anglers know, by the time such a stream reaches the foot of the mountains, it may be unable to sustain trout year-round. But even under ordinary circumstances, a freestone river is a pretty hard world—with extreme and often rapid fluctuations in water level, with swings in temperature from near-freezing water in winter to the tepid flows of high summer, with scouring currents that flush rich organic material downstream and keep portions of the channel scrubbed to bare bedrock.

What anglers call spring creeks answer to the same invariable dynamics of gravity and friction, pressure and resistance, but they present a markedly different character. Typically, spring creeks flow through low-gradient, though not necessarily low-altitude, terrain—among meadows or rolling hills, along valley floors, in high-desert rangeland, on volcanic plateaus, or over broad floodplains eroded by larger rivers that are not themselves spring creeks. Many of these landscapes are composed in part of fine erosional sediments, and the soils may be deeper, richer, and less rocky than those found in the mountains, though the greater variety of spring-creek watersheds makes any generalizations about them subject to exception. On flatter land, rain and snowmelt drain off more slowly, giving them greater opportunity to percolate down through layers of soil and replenish the groundwater. The gentler topography and the capacity of porous underlying rock to absorb water act as buffers against the heavy surface runoff that can raise a tiny mountain creek to a full torrent in remarkably short order. Even when a spring creek is bank-full from melting snow or prolonged rain, the low gradient of the land keeps the current speed low and minimizes scouring floods. As a result, rich organic matter provided by decaying vegetation remains in the stream and available as food for a variety of creatures; and aquatic plants, not a feature of most mountain waters, have a chance to take root. A spring creek, like a freestone river, does maintain its volume in part with water entering the channel in subsurface flow from shallow layers of soil. But to a far greater extent than in mountain streams, spring creeks are recharged by true groundwater.

Springs, or at least some of them, occur at all because the water table is not flat. It follows, though very approximately, the contour of the surface land. It can be higher beneath a hill or rise, since water infiltrating through the soil makes its way rather slowly down to the saturated rock of an aquifer. The downward flow that would tend to flatten the water table is hindered, as the water must find its way through the tiny spaces between particles of soil, small crevices, or pores in the rock. Rainwater falling on a hill can "stack up," producing a hump in the water table, though not as pronounced as the hill above it. The slope of the water table seldom exceeds 2 degrees, which doesn't sound like much, but over distances it can add up and produce a significant differential in elevation. If the water table slopes gently downward from the crest of a hill and the hillside angles down more steeply, the two surfaces will meet, often at the very toe of the hill. Wherever the saturated underground rock is exposed, groundwater flows to the surface. In most instances, it seeps out inconspicuously, and it is not unusual around spring creeks to find small, perpetually marshy patches along the bank where groundwater leaches out and into the stream. Where the geologic material of the aquifer contains irregularities—fissures, faults, joints, seams—groundwater takes the path of least resistance and flows through these less-restricted avenues, sometimes in a volume great enough to produce the bubbling of a spring. For the most part these are small enough that the distinction between a seep and a spring is only a matter of terminology. But sometimes, sufficient water flows to make a spring quite visible, and occasionally, a stream may issue full-blown and all at once from a single spring of substantial size. These, however, are unusual, and most springs are apt to be far less dramatic—a little bubbling at the stream edge or a tiny roil in shallow water. And some groundwater enters a spring creek by filtering directly into the channel, much like a hole dug in the beach will fill with water that seeps almost imperceptibly through the sand. Wherever the bottom of the stream channel is lower than the surface of the water table, this kind of infiltration will occur. In some places, the flow of water up through the streambed may be strong enough to keep the stream gravels free of silt and aquatic vegetation, creating a reach of cool, upwelling water that makes ideal spawning habitat for trout.

Groundwater must be replenished by rain and snow, but an aquifer is in a very real sense a reservoir, since water-saturated rock releases its contents gradually. The speed with which water moves through an aquifer varies with the kind of geologic material, though one hydrologist suggests that one hundred feet or so per year is a typical figure. This slow rate of travel smooths out local fluctuations in the water supply. The lag time tends to stabilize the release of water, metering it out at a fairly constant rate, and groundwater will continue to flow even during dry periods and replenish a spring creek in times when a freestone stream might be reduced to a series of lukewarm, stagnant pools. A water table that lies deeper than ten feet underground, as most do, is effectively insulated from seasonal variations of heat and cold at the surface, and the groundwater assumes the temperature of the surrounding rock. In the northern temperate zone, springs and seeps flow year-round at about fifty to fifty-five degrees and keep a stream cool during the summer and warm during the winter. And under the right geological conditions—ones in fact that are implicit in an angler's definition of a spring creek—groundwater passing through an aquifer will dissolve minerals from the soil and rock along its path and transport them to the stream, where they replenish the chemical fertility necessary to aquatic life.

Fishermen most often associate spring creeks with a limestone geology, and in fact one hears the term "limestoner" used locally to denote this type of stream. Limestone is formed of carbonate minerals, which dissolve in the presence of even weak acids, though solubility depends upon the particular form of limestone. Calcite, one common type, is highly soluble; dolomite, another widespread form, high in magnesium, is less so. As precipitation falls through the atmosphere, it picks up carbon dioxide, and by the time it reaches the ground, even "pure" rainwater is mildly acidic. Passing through an aquifer, this water reacts with the limestone, increases in pH, and transfers dissolved carbonates to the stream through a spring or seep. This chemical enrichment promotes the growth of aquatic life, from tiny organisms to crustaceans to plants, and gives spring creeks their phenomenal biological productivity. At the same time, a high pH causes toxic heavy metals to precipitate out as relatively harmless compounds and maintains a consistent, stable water chemistry. Limestone trout streams are scattered here and there across North America but approach something like real abundance in only two, fairly restricted geographic localities—southwest Wisconsin (and the bordering edges of Minnesota, Iowa, and Illinois) and south-central Pennsylvania—landscapes that, perhaps unsurprisingly, bear striking resemblance to one another. The Pennsylvania waters are certainly the better known and among the most celebrated in American angling. In part because these eastern waters were some of the first encountered by Europeans, and in part because of a certain geological similarity to the English chalkstreams—arguably the richest trout habitat to be found in moving water—limestone streams have become the archetypal form of spring creek in America.

But an entirely different set of geological conditions can in fact lay the foundation for spring creeks. Under the right circumstances, volcanic basalt can produce an aquifer that is functionally similar to limestone. The enormous quantities of steam and gas that accompany a volcanic eruption may become mixed in the solidifying magma, producing a rock riddled with tiny voids and hollows that absorb water. Water moving through fractures and joints that develop as the rock cools will emerge as a spring, and many of the spring creeks in Idaho are of this type. Some volcanic events are dramatically explosive and blow vast clouds of silica-rich ash into the air. The ash cools rapidly to a form of volcanic glass; it traps air and gas as it settles and eventually compacts to porous rock, through which water may migrate. Hot Creek in the Eastern Sierra of California, I am told, and the Firehole River in Yellowstone originated this way.

Volcanic formations may not produce mechanisms of water storage and transmission quite as ideal as those in limestone or chalk, but they compensate in other ways. Basalt flows may spread over huge areas, and the extensive capture surface for precipitation helps recharge groundwater in regions that are often arid. Water travels great distances through the rock, and this long pipeline maintains a stable flow at the spring. Silica-rich volcanic products may be faulted, and water moves down these faults to a substantial depth, appearing at the surface after a long underground migration. The result, again, is a spring of relatively constant volume, very much like a limestone creek. Unlike limestone, basalt does not contain calcium carbonate; it is, however, high in calcium and magnesium and reacts with groundwater to produce a stream with a high pH. Calcium concentrations are much lower in silica ash but still sufficient to produce calcium-rich water with a chemistry and quality approaching that of a limestone stream.

One other geological configuration can produce a spring creek, or at least a spring-creek-like stream. Large rivers create broad floodplains, and over time they shift their course from side to side across the plain, withdrawing from old channels and cutting off oxbows as they move. An abandoned channel may maintain a flow of water from a spring or seep in the floodplain gravels, forming a spring-creek tributary to the main river. The volume may fluctuate somewhat more than is typical of other spring creeks, and the pH of the water will be high only if the pH of the main river is high, but the resulting stream may be virtually indistinguishable from spring creeks of other origins. Spring-fed floodplain streams like this exist in, among other places, Alberta and Montana.

Limestone and volcanic rock could hardly be more different. Limestone is sedimentary, animal in origin, produced by a long-term accumulation on ocean floors. Volcanic rocks are igneous, emphatically mineral, sudden and violent creations. Limestone is born in water, volcanic rock in fire. Yet the streams they give rise to are strikingly similar: stable, year-round flows of spring water, constant in temperature and volume; a consistent and gentle streambed gradient that permits the accumulation of biological nutrients and the rooting of aquatic vegetation; an underlying geology that tempers the effects of heavy rain and runoff; a steady and favorable chemistry that promotes the growth of plant and animal life; a habitat that varies little as the world around it succumbs to the changing seasons.

~~~~~~~~~~

Resilient and reliable, richly constituted, quietly hospitable and productive, consistent in the face of extremes—such qualities are as rare in a trout stream as they are in people, though this is a fact I failed to appreciate for quite some time. For the first half of my life, I fished pretty much where I grew up, and I grew up where I was born, in an area of low, undulating hills and broad expanses of farmland on the border between Wisconsin and Illinois. In the matter of trout streams, I was inexperienced and uninformed, a blinkered parochial who fished neither widely nor well—only often, with great enthusiasm, and almost exclusively in the small spring creeks scattered throughout the southwest corner of Wisconsin. All my notions about trout and trout water derived entirely from these little brooks, which, I would come to discover, were typical enough as spring creeks go but phenomenally unrepresentative of trout streams in general. That fish and moving water elsewhere might behave otherwise never once occurred to me.

In my early twenties, I left the Midwest—for good, as it turned out, though I did not know this at the time—and what I'd imagined as provisional, short-term relocation somehow grew into an eight-year residence at the foot of the Blue Ridge Mountains in Virginia. When trout season opened that first spring, I fished, with some difficulty, my first freestone stream, a lively creek doglegging down a mountainside covered in hardwood forest. Though the trees were not yet in leaf, the bare limbs of redbud sprouted popcornlike clusters of pink blossoms, and lower in the understory dogwood flowered. Against the backdrop of naked branches, these blooms produced the most wonderful impression that they floated, disembodied, in the air. On the forest floor, not yet green, wood anemone, bloodroot, and trillium grew in small stands, and perfectly shaped, leafless bouquets of bluets sprang from bare patches of sand along the bank. I made my way upstream, not altogether certain how to fish this unfamiliar water, not sure I was doing it right, catching only a small brook trout here and there from the most obvious places. Then I stumbled on a minor jackpot, a brisk channel nearly waist-deep beside a block of stone the size of a toolshed that had split from a rock face and toppled in the stream. It was full of fish and became, that first spring, my ace in the hole, the one spot where I could always take a decent trout or two. And I started to think I'd made some headway sorting out this strange, fast, stony water, so unlike the spring creeks of home.

I also began to see that the rest of one's life, the parts that don't fish—citizen; employee; taxpayer; I, the undersigned—will somehow always know when trout season opens and time their demands accordingly. I didn't manage to get fishing again until after midsummer, the forest canopy now thick and green and shady, poison ivy everywhere, and my ace shrunken to a deuce, a shallow and troutless trickle. I'd never before seen a river waste away, dry to a skeleton of rocky ribs and vertebrae poking through a desiccated skin. And this dispiriting turn of affairs only grew worse. By fall, even the trickle had vanished, and the stream seemed less water than sun-bleached stone, no longer defined by where it was, but by where it used to be. I never did figure out where all the trout went. Changes like this force you to adapt and improvise and, I suppose, to become a better fisherman. But as far as the stream itself is concerned, you learn to keep your guard up. Even now, though I fish freestone rivers most of the time, I can never do so without troubling myself beforehand with worries of high water or low, too warm or too cold, where the fish might be today or tomorrow. Such water is not to be trusted.

Spring creeks change too, of course, but their fluctuations tend to be less extreme and of shorter duration. High water from heavy rains may last only hours or days rather than weeks; high summer heat may warm the creek, but never to bathwater. Some elasticity in the system draws the stream back to a certain equilibrium, which is possible at all because a spring creek has a fixed identity in the first place. But on a freestone river everything is negotiable. A mountain stream is never high or low, only high or low for the time of year. It is mercurial by nature; it giveth and it taketh away, its identity shifting and contingent, its trout now here, now there, depending. Even so, some water and often a good deal of it is plainly fishless, too shallow, or exposed, or too short of cover and so of little interest. And just as obvious are the prime places, the pools and runs, riffles and pockets that unquestionably hold trout. I don't mean to suggest that a freestone river fishes more easily than a spring creek (they pose somewhat different problems) or that it is in some way physically less complicated (it is probably more so), but only that the structure of a mountain stream is largely self-evident, a direct translation of the surrounding rock into the language of currents and calms. It is a creature of surfaces, answering always to an underlying geology, mineral in color and smell, water lapping stone with precise and unequivocal borders that divide one from the other. A mountain stream flows emphatically over the land.

A spring creek, on the other hand, is embedded in the land, running through rather than over its more tractable soils, the currents less haphazard, more measured, as though its flowing were a considered response. It is an architecture of banks, not bottom, at once oddly independent of its substrate yet wholly contiguous with the land around it. To wade a freestone stream is to walk on the crust of the earth; step into a spring creek and you may find yourself knee-deep, and still sinking, in loose suspensions of sand and silt that make it difficult to say exactly what or where the bottom is. A spring creek has boundaries but not barriers; at its edges, the water does not suddenly stop but shades to wetness in tangles of roots and rootlets and in masses of half-submerged watercress, and then becomes mud that trails off to dampness in the soil beyond. In there somewhere, dry land begins. Or the current may undercut the soft streamside loam, nibbling inward and underground to leave a shelf of earth and vegetation extending over the water, blurring any clear division between the creek and its bank. Everywhere, a spring creek bleeds and blends into the land around it, and except for the very largest ones, which are rare—an anomaly among anomalies—a spring creek is almost all edge, favoring depth over width. Fishing, like fish, and like much in the natural world, flourishes at the edges of things, and on a good spring creek, there are trout almost everywhere. The banks lie close together, subtracting the water of least appeal, those broad expanses of middle, to leave only a lush and irresistible periphery that goes on and on. The channel meanders in riparian switchbacks, and for every mile the crow flies, a spring creek runs three.

In the end, a freestone river is a transcript of surfaces. Written by bedrock and boulder, it is the most legible of all waters, its anatomy unambiguous and literal. And while even the clearest pools easily conceal fish, the stream itself feels somehow too transparent for the sense of mystery or surprise that lies at the heart of fishing and the love of landscape. Mountain streams have their wonders, of course; the simple fact of trout is enough to guarantee it. But even the tiniest spring creek possesses a certain interior quality, some dimension or place, a "deep within" that I have never known on freestone rivers large or small. I live near mountain waters now, and love them immensely as places to fish, but less so simply as places.

It is difficult to account for the discrepancy. While our link to a specific place may be readily explained, the origin of our attachment to a type of place, to a particular arrangement of landforms and watercourses, species and mixes of plants and animals, to indigenous shapes and colors and textures, is anything but clear. Every acre of earth represents an accident of geology, climate, and, more often than not, of human intervention; that one specific form of accident—a spring-creek landscape, for instance—should appeal above all others seems itself accidental. It is not a matter of some built-in aesthetic character. Nature is nowhere inherently beautiful; we only invest it with beauty—a fact that by no means reduces the power or pleasure we feel, but one that raises questions about why we distribute those investments unequally.

The attraction to certain landscapes feels at times intrinsic enough to be biological, a proclivity coiled in our genes before birth. We come into the world, for whatever reason, already equipped with individual propensities, small pieces of the person we will one day become. And though it may not be likely, it is not impossible either that our predilection for a form of landscape is like an aptitude for music, or a fear of heights, or a quickness with numbers, or a love of risk—an innate constituent. It certainly appears sometimes to inhabit us at this level. I have friends who moved to the West, where they instantly and utterly, and in some cases literally, took to the mountains, as though life to that point had been a mere preliminary to claiming a landscape they'd never laid eyes on before. For others, it was the high desert or the Pacific coast or the Alaskan outback, but always the affinity between person and place was so sure and automatic that it looked to be inherent. Psychologists, geographers, and other academic types, in the brief interludes between clubbing one another for stipends, have sought links between landscape and human nature, but predictably have cast little light on the matter. Still, I find myself hoping that such a connection exists, that the cause of our attraction to place is as deeply ingrained as the effect. In the end, however, it may be more likely that the bond grows from history rather than biology, though I'm not sure that this so much explains things as simply identifies a different kind of mystery. An image of place implanted by chance—a photograph seen, a book read, a story heard—takes root and flowers in the strange soil of the heart, a garden-variety case of love at first sight.

A few years ago, a friend who is both a fine fly fisherman and an accomplished essayist wrote to me about his home water, the Kennebec River in Maine, and tried to explain that strange form of gravity that draws us to a place. It is a lovely river (I have seen it since), and his letter did justice to its many charms. Aware, however, that the whole in such matters will forever exceed the sum of its parts, that essences invariably prove elusive and incommunicable, he could finally offer only this accounting: "There is that certain way in which all fishing places are one of two things, with no intervening possibilities: they are either completely sufficient, or they aren't." And I think this is all that can be said about landscapes as well. The nature of their sufficiency is too fugitive to capture in words, though it leaves a trail everywhere, a quality felt simply as "enough." The consequence is a kind of completeness that abolishes any distinction between what happened and where. Place and experience become reciprocal touchstones, each authenticating the other. The landscape swells with the meaning of what has been lived there, and the shape of that living has, in turn, been molded by the place. The landscape no longer exists as a backdrop or setting but as a medium of experience, a material from which the occasion is fashioned, a character in the story of a life.

To me, spring-creek country has been a place of just this kind. And though trout fishing has inevitably been involved, sometimes at the center of things, sometimes only around the edges, fishing has never been more than a part of it all, a necessary but not sufficient condition. For the central mystery of spring creeks is not the trout but the springs themselves. That clear, cold water should issue from the ground, spontaneously and continuously, is to me a most extraordinary thing, as it was to people of the past. It was once thought that streams flowed magically from a vast subterranean ocean—a belief at least properly scaled to the marvel of moving water and, in its largest outline, one not terribly far from the truth. To regard springs as we do now, as the relief valves for a complex mechanism of water capture and underground storage, molecular migration and pressure differentials does not at all explain away their wonder. It is often the case that technical accounts of natural phenomena are even more fantastic than the conceptions they displace, and what was once merely remarkable becomes, in the light of science, nearly incredible. That a great many cultures have endowed springs with numinous properties—curative power, rebirth and regeneration, prophesy and oracle—is scarcely surprising, and that they would have been regarded as sacred seems almost inevitable. Water is an ancient emblem of spiritual purification, and its symbolic power to absolve is as old as the need to be forgiven. That spring water is now bottled and labeled and successfully hawked for more than the price of milk or gasoline may not be the lunacy of late capitalism that it first appears. Springs return to the surface water that may have bled slowly and unseen through underground rock for years or decades or centuries, the aftermath of long ago still making itself felt. A spring is the past unearthed, issuing from a crack in time. In its waters old stories are told, a disclosure of hidden workings flowing like an open vein or welling up to the skin of the earth like blood in a bruise.

Every existence has its pulse points, those places where life rises somehow closer to the surface and makes itself more sharply felt. Spring creeks have been mine. Like a revelation or like a wound, they have more immediately registered the heart of things. It was on a spring creek in the Midwest that I first learned to love a landscape in a way that went beyond my use for it, where I came to see that possessing a place was not the same as owning it. I courted my wife on a spring creek in Virginia, winning her, I like to think, on a hot and windy August afternoon when I secretly swept a grasshopper from the tall weeds and sidearmed it into the water. "Watch there," I said and pointed, just as it disappeared in the quick rise of a brown trout. I believe she thought, just for an instant, that I'd conjured a fish with the wave of a hand, and turning in astonishment, laughing, she said, "Do that again."

On another August day, along a spring creek in Wisconsin, my two brothers and I, soon to go our separate ways, sat on a grassy bank in the small shade of a cornfield and talked of what might come next. A season later, two of us came again to the same spot, this time with no words to speak, sitting in a silent grief for the empty place beside us, mourning a brother who would never return, wondering how it could be that absence, that a thing not even there, could fill up so much space.

In an old stone house overlooking a Pennsylvania spring creek, my soon-to-be wife and I gathered with friends to celebrate our engagement. There was a total solar eclipse, and the birds quieted down as though it were night. That afternoon I saw a swarm of honeybees in a small plum tree, clustered so thickly that they bent the slender limb nearly to breaking, a hanging teardrop of solid bodies that produced the most wonderful sound. Next morning they were gone, but the party went on for five days. Just before moving west, I fished a spring creek one last evening with friends who were as vital to me as oxygen, and though I stayed around for a couple more days, that night was the real parting. Three months and three thousand miles later, my wife and I, worn ragged with the business of starting a new life, slipped away with forged travel papers, eluded surveillance, and escaped to a spring creek in Oregon, where we got our first good look at this place we would call home. I threw fat golden stoneflies to eager little rainbow trout, but she was on to the trick by then.

A few years later and much too soon, the longing to see my father and the rage at his death, suspended in the necessity of living, overtook me at last on a spring creek in England that too closely evoked the small stream where he'd first taught me about fishing. The nettle and wild onion were in bloom, and I remember it was a Thursday. Half a world away and six seasons afterward, on a spring creek in Montana, I passed a rare morning with a rare companion, the kind of generous and gentle soul, like my father, that you are sometimes lucky enough to meet. We sat at the favorite bend of his favorite pool, waiting for a hatch of pale morning duns, talking of this and that, cultivating a friendship that still thrives. I privately hoped that no mayflies would show up and interrupt us, and they didn't.

I cannot recall these times, or a thousand others, apart from the spring creeks themselves, for there is no essential difference between the intimacy of occasion and the intimacy of place. They share the same secret interior, and it has never appeared to me that it could be otherwise.

I first learned to fish, then to fish trout, then to fly fish on spring creeks, and it is a truism among anglers that the deepest affections attach to first waters. They become our private archetypes. We treasure them in the beginning because they are all we know, and then afterward because they are familiar and perhaps because we fish them better and might measure how far we've come. And still later, when catching means less than it once did, we love them for the depth and richness of their associations. The images of people, the reflections of other times and places are mirrored in a silver surface, and fishing becomes a form of memory, and memory a form of return.

2

Driftless

~~~~~~~~~~

What is the self but the sum of everything we remember?
—**Milan Kundera, *The Book of Laughter and Forgetting***

Words are, among other things, instruments of domestication, a way of laying claim to a thing, of taming something wild and making it our own. To give a name to a place is to plant a flag or to leave a kind of cultural footprint on the land. And sometimes the reciprocal also occurs: a place turns around and leaves a stamp of its own on the language. The island-nation off the coast of India that we now know as Sri Lanka, and knew as Ceylon before that, was for a long time called Serendib, an Arabic term that extends at least as far back as the fourth century and is itself a corruption of an even earlier Sanskrit word. The Arabic name was widely used in the West, perhaps an inevitable consequence of the covetous eye that Europe has always trained on the lands of North Africa and the Middle East. In 1754, British man of letters Horace Walpole, inspired by a Persian fairy tale in which three princes of the island continually make unanticipated, chance discoveries, coined the term "serendipity." That a word signifying unforeseen, fortunate accidents should have its roots in a remote and romantic land seems to me exactly right. It is how the best places are usually found.

By the age of fourteen, I had already acquired a reputation of sorts as an avid fisherman, and like most public perceptions, this one was not strictly accurate. Passionate about fishing to the point of fanatical, I'd read and reread and virtually memorized every shred of information I could lay my hands on, from books and magazines, newspapers and encyclopedias, tackle catalogs and travel brochures. And I think it fair to say that for my age and circumstances I was uncommonly well informed, even about types of angling I had not yet done—jigging for walleye, surfcasting, flats fishing, salmon mooching, handlining North Atlantic cod, drift-fishing steelhead—as well as types I still haven't done—bluewater trolling for tuna, snagging paddlefish, noodling catfish, chumming shark, and harpooning sailfish. But most of this knowledge remained abstract and hypothetical; my own only hands-on experience was confined to fishing lakes for panfish and bass, coarse-fishing little creeks, and a single day I spent, woozy with motion sickness, soaking bait from a party boat off the coast of Florida and catching nothing. The vast gulf between theory and practice didn't trouble me much—an attitude, no doubt, that inevitably led me later to a career in academics—but I longed to fish more and most especially to fly fish for trout, though I appreciated the reality that "fly fishing" and "trout" in fact represented two different aspirations, which would need to be addressed one at a time. I thought trout the most elegant, even exotic, of creatures, just far enough beyond the edge of my experience to hold the intrigue of remoteness, just near enough not to be impossible. At night, like Thoreau, I dreamed of trout fishing.

In this frame of mind and by sheer accident, I happened to cross paths with a casual acquaintance of my older sister's. His first name, as I recall, was John, but I'm not entirely certain since everyone called him by his last—Hawker—a practice he at least tacitly encouraged by never correcting anyone. I believe he liked the name, its edgy Dashiell Hammett sound, the distant intimation of predatory menace, the name of a man who could handle himself. I in turn enjoyed the dispensation to address an older person by his surname, a rare liberty at that time of life when social distinctions based upon age are inflexible and tyrannically enforced. Moreover, Hawker possessed the two most enviable commodities a fourteen-year-old could imagine: a driver's license and the wheels to go with it. Never a serious gearhead, I was nonetheless awed by Hawker's ride. The heyday of big Detroit musclemobiles had peaked, but only just, and was being subsumed bit by bit into the national obsession for overpowered luxury. In this shifting automotive climate, Hawker acquired an immaculate new GTO, lacquered a blindingly glossy, in-your-face, hot tangerine and tricked out in all the appurtenances of coolness: an ominous stripe painted down its length; ram-air intake; enormous, wide tires with white lettering; four-barrel carburetion; twin chrome exhausts; a stylish T-handled walnut shift knob; and eight-track tape. Obscenely horsepowered, it idled with the rumbling, throaty gurgle of a racing boat.

I may have been young, but certain ironies were not lost on me, and I found it odd that those two fundamental emblems of American identity, one's name and one's car, should in this case so poorly fit their owner. For despite an occasional impulse to throttle the orange beast to alarming speeds, shut off the ignition, and quickly restart it just to hear the engine backfire, Hawker was almost pathologically reserved and soft-spoken—characteristics thrown into still greater relief by his size. Even at the age of seventeen, he was a hulking presence, or so I remember him, but I don't believe there was a malicious bone in his prepossessing, bearlike frame. Instead, there was something else, a kind of distractedness or preoccupation about him. While he always stared directly at you when he spoke, in that intense and unnerving way that some people have, he never really made eye contact. It felt more like he was looking at something you couldn't see, directly behind and far beyond you. I came to find out that Hawker's grandfather, a man with whom he was very close, had died recently, and at the time I attributed his demeanor to sorrow over his grandfather's passing. It was another ten years, long after we had parted ways, before I would understand in his manner not simply grief, but the haunted apprehensiveness of one who still falls asleep to the dread of a midnight phone call and has learned, as one does, that the call can come just as easily at midday. I never knew the details of Hawker's story. Perhaps there were none beyond the sad and ordinary death of an old man, yet it always seemed as though there might have been more. Either way, his loss occasioned our brief friendship.

Hawker's grandfather had apparently been an avid angler and, the evidence suggested, fished the fly at least part of the time. He had also maintained some sort of log or journal, which I recognized from my reading was something that all serious anglers did. I never understood precisely whether he revealed the contents of this journal to his grandson sometime during his last days, or whether Hawker discovered the volume among his effects afterward. The account, vague to begin with, changed from one telling to the next, and this inconsistency, along with repeatedly unmet assurances that I could inspect the book (or books; again the details were murky) led me to suspect for a while that he'd simply fabricated the whole thing. But in the end a handful of highly specific details proved so accurate that I subsequently had no doubt that the document actually existed. I would trade my best fly rod for a look at it now, not to sift it for fishing secrets but only to get some insight into this man who knew the waters I came to love and fished them at a time before I was born.

According to Hawker, the log referred at various points to a certain trout stream, a spring creek in southwestern Wisconsin, and went on to describe a particular pool (there may have even been a rough sketch of its location) where his grandfather had found fishing memorable enough to preserve in his notes. The old man apparently made no mention of specific fish or general size or numbers, so I naturally assumed, as anglers tend to, that the trout were so large and abundant that no written tally was needed to call them to mind. But he did record his secret weapon—a fly-rod Flatfish, a tight-wiggling little plug shaped like a smashed banana, so tiny and light that casting it could be effected only with fly tackle. I knew the lure well but didn't have one, which was immaterial anyway since I didn't own a fly rod either, and I look back now in some relief at the thousand treble-hook-related tragedies that were thereby averted. The journal also named a small town near the stream, and once we'd scrounged up a map, it became no great matter to get a general sense of its vicinity. A week or so later, Hawker fueled up his battle-cruiser and we set off.

I caught one fish that day. Without much experience to go on, I retrieved from my varied readings a scrap of wisdom from the masters: fish the places that other anglers overlook. So I considered the matter, baited up, then lowered a worm into the rushing black throat of a corrugated steel culvert that funneled the stream under a country road. Moments later, I snaked out from beneath the asphalt the first trout I had ever caught—an undignified extraction that cemented my faith in the complete infallibility of the written word and simultaneously disabused me of the long-held notion that brown trout were actually brown.

The story is ordinary enough, I suppose, but it lingers in memory because it accorded so perfectly with the romantic notions that I held about trout streams and fishing—the musty journal, the secret stream, the twilit ground between fact and myth. Hawker and I fished together only once more—I don't believe he finally took to it much—and we hunted pheasants a time or two, which never took hold of me, and I can't say that I ever knew him well. He remained one of those people who, from time to time, drift inside the periphery of a life and midwife some change, more a catalyst than a material component of the reaction, and then just as quietly drift out again. But in that short time, a door had opened, and while I may have lifted the latch, Hawker had turned the key. What lay beyond was ten thousand square miles of trout country.

≈≈≈≈≈≈≈≈≈

The southwest corner of Wisconsin—a rough right triangle of land bounded by Illinois on the south, the Mississippi River on the west, and an irregular line extending from north of La Crosse to a point just west of Beloit—encloses more than just an arbitrary space within geopolitical boundaries. It represents a distinct physiographic region, an area defined by its specific surface geography, and were you to drive there, you wouldn't need a map to know when you'd arrived. It simply looks different. Come into it from any direction, but particularly from the east, and you can't help but notice, just beyond

Madison, a change in the landscape. Behind you, over broad flats and gentle swells, the highways run straight as strings, often in grids that mark the township-and-range planning of a frontier explicitly surveyed for settlement. The farms, some now subdivided or consolidated or plowed into anonymity by the surging engines of modern agribusiness, still suggest the faint checkerboard of the original 160-acre quarter sections. Towns are strategically sited, platted in the last century by a succession of commercial interests: fur trading, lumber and pulp, agriculture, the railroads.

Ahead of you, though, the land begins to wrinkle and fold, like a fingerprint or the creases in an old man's palm, producing an almost regular alternation of steep-sided ridges and small, deep ravines locally called "coulees," an old and relict name from the first French exploration of the region. Two-lane blacktops, shoulderless and unlined, rise and fall with the terrain, twisting around sidehills and coiling down the valleys. The farms are smaller here, confined to the narrow plateaus and flatter ridge tops and scattered irregularly along meandering strips of bottomland; the slopes that rise from valley floors, too steep to till, remain in mixed hardwood forest. Towns grow fewer, giving way to villages and unincorporated hamlets. Some were originally located for convenience in a land where travel was slow; some were situated by default at the terminus of dead-end railroad spurs where the terrain was too rough to continue a through line. Some rose from squatters' land, where Cornish immigrants first mined lead, Yorkshiremen smelted it, and others dripped molten metal from wooden shot towers to feed an emerging nation's endless appetite for war, first against the original inhabitants, then against kings who claimed the new world, and finally, when no one else was left, against itself. And some settlements were merely invented from nothing by land speculators who planted stakes in the ground and hoped

a town would grow. Usually, it didn't. And to an extent surprising in the modern world, the region has so far escaped the
unappeasable gluttony of real-estate development, which,
not far away, has ingested landscapes whole; devoured farms,
trees, and rivers; extracted the cash; and left behind only its
excrement: destination shopping malls; grim expanses of
identical three-bedroom ranchburgers; ludicrous, overscaled
McMansions on quarter-acre plots, huddled in enclaves
deliriously named "Oak Creek Vista Estates," though there
are no oaks, creeks, vistas, or estates; and landfills to hold the
husks of all the needs that proved fraudulent. Such things
will arrive in time, I imagine; no place can hold out indefinitely against "growth," even when in reality it is only me-
tastasis. But for the time being, many of the old farmsteads
remain, cell phones and pagers have yet to become the chief
instruments of human contact, springs run clear, and the
ridges and hillsides still look blue in the evening light. To descend into any one of a hundred small valleys feels a bit like
going back in time because, in a sense, you are.

Two million years ago, shifting tectonic forces rearranged
the world's landmasses in a way that isolated the oceans at
high latitudes from those at lower ones and prevented the
once free exchange of water between polar and tropical seas.
Patterns of seasonal temperature fluctuation changed, and
the planet entered the third and most recent of its three great
glacial ages. During such a time, the climate does not grow
uniformly cold but rather responds to a shorter, 100,000-year
astronomical cycle based on the shape of the earth's orbit, its
axial tilt, and the season of the year in which it comes closest
to the sun. This cycle produces, within the long glacial age,
comparatively cool periods of glaciation when the ice cover
of the earth expands, alternating with relatively warm, interglacial ages when the ice recedes. We are, in fact, currently
living in an interglacial period, a temporary interval of warm-

ing that reached its peak 10,000 years ago and is now more than half over. The ice will return, then retreat, again and again, and if those who construct such histories can be trusted, these cycles will continue for another 8 million years.

There have already been four major glaciations during the last million years or so of the present glacial age, each covering virtually all of Canada and the northern United States with an ice cap the size of Antarctica. And though differing in configuration, geographical reach, and duration, each glaciation rearranged the work of the previous one and profoundly remade the surface geography. The most recent event, termed the Wisconsinan glaciation for its southernmost advance, began about 65,000 years ago and ended only recently, about 12,000 years ago, or roughly the time that human beings arrived in North America. This last glaciation sculpted the landscape of the upper Midwest into its present shape.

The power necessary to structure such vast topographies is almost inconceivable. To envision a glacier by observing an ice field in the Rockies or an expanse of frozen tundra is like trying to infer a hurricane from a sneeze. Glaciers do not develop like the freezing surface of a pond or the sprouting of an icicle. They do not materialize, they move in. Or, more accurately, they are pushed. A glacier forms when, over a long period of time, annual snowfall exceeds annual snowmelt. With each year's residual accumulation, the snow cap grows larger and deeper, and under the pressure of increasing weight, the lowermost layers of snow consolidate into ice. As more snow falls, the ice becomes thicker, until a dome of snow builds so high and heavy that the ice beneath it is squeezed outward at the edges and begins to slide over the surface of the land. But the edge of the glacier does not always advance uniformly; it may be influenced by local landforms that encourage the ice to move through some areas while hampering it in others, and the glacier may eventually flow in tongue-shaped lobes. All of this takes place on an enormous scale. The lobe of ice that extended over Wisconsin in the last glaciation was a mile thick in places, driven by the weight of a 10,000-foot snow dome centered in an area northwest of Hudson's Bay.

Such a glacier may inch along or periodically surge and move a mile a year, but in either case the force is enough to shear off hilltops and fill in valleys. It may cut new river channels and obliterate old ones. It transports rock and soil over long distances; enormous boulders bearing the native copper of Michigan's Upper Peninsula have been discovered as far south as Illinois, and diamonds from fields in Canada turn up from time to time in Wisconsin. A glacier bulldozes the earth ahead of it or molds it beneath into the whale-shaped mounds of drumlins. The sheer mass of the ice depresses the crust of the earth, as much as three thousand feet at the peak of the last glaciation. Rock freezes to the underside, forming a coarse, abrasive surface that scrapes, gouges, and polishes the land beneath it; it crushes stone to gravel and pulverizes gravel to a powder so fine that geologists call it "rock flour."

The power of an advancing glacier is matched perhaps only by the power of a receding one. A glacier doesn't retreat in the sense of moving backward; it melts, and massive quantities of ice produce equally massive amounts of water. Huge rivers form underneath, on top of, and inside the ice, and like any rivers, they carry vast loads of sediment and lay them down in broad outwash plains. Ice temporarily dams some rivers, creating great glacial lakes, where sand and silt settle evenly on the bottom, remaining flat and smooth when the ice dam breaks and the water drains away. Holes develop in the rotting glacial lobe, sucking down whirlpools of water, rock, and soil, and depositing them in the earthen cones of kames; subglacial streams drop sand and gravel into the snaky, narrow ridges of eskers. Great blocks of stagnant ice, broken off from the underside of the glacier and covered with outwash, slowly melt into deep kettle lakes. Relieved of the terrific weight of ice, the surface of the earth begins to spring back to its original elevation; it is still rebounding today, at the rate of half an inch a year in places.

What is left in the wake of a retreating glacier is "drift"— the rubble of glacial till plowed up by the edges of the ice into the long, low ridges of moraines; rock, gravel, and silt, frozen to the underside of the glacier and laid down on the land when the ice melts; geologic material carried inside or atop the glacier and deposited when the ice sheet shrinks. And this drift forms an entirely new landscape everywhere.

Everywhere, that is, except southwest Wisconsin. During as many as fifteen successive glaciations over the course of a million years, the ice cap never once intruded into this small corner of the world. Its glacial history is a string of near misses, though why this should be so is not entirely clear. It may have been a consequence of topography. The low basin of Lake Superior and the highlands bordering its southern edge may have diverted glaciers to the east and west, like a boulder splitting floodwaters. Or it may simply have been chance, an accident, serendipity. Whatever the cause, this southwest portion of the state time and again escaped the leveling effect of advancing ice, a circumstance as unlikely as standing in a thundershower and somehow remaining bone-dry. There are none of the signature landforms here—no moraines or eskers, few natural lakes, no outwash plains or expanses of drift that shaped the surrounding countryside. It is a landscape negatively defined, most notable not for what happened but for what didn't. The glaciers left their footprint in the reverse impression of a name—the driftless area—and the landscape here dates to a much older time.

More than a billion years ago, in what would become the upper Midwest, an often violent geological history of volcanic eruptions and tectonic events that heaved up mountains as high as the Alps came to an end. A long period of weathering ensued, wearing down the high ground and infilling the low, a leveling that produced some of the oldest sedimentary rock in North America. The crust of the earth then began to subside, gradually sinking into itself deeply enough to allow an ancient ocean to advance over the land. The sea was tropical; the continents were still fused in the great landmass of Pangaea, and the paleoequator crossed the driftless area. On the leading edge of this marine intrusion, wave action and currents distributed eroded material into beds of sandstone hundreds of feet thick on the sea floor. As water continued to move over the land, areas once shallow grew deeper, and in offshore zones the bodies of countless tiny, lime-secreting organisms accumulated on the ocean bottom to form a layer of dolomite over the sandstone. After a time, the earth's crust began to warp upward, the sea floor slowly rose, and the water became increasingly shallow until finally the ocean bottom was once again dry land.

Over the course of the next 500 million years or so, this cycle of marine transgression and regression repeated itself several times, each event similar in general characteristics but unique in its details—the composition of the intruding sea, its depth and reach and duration, the speed of advance and withdrawal. And each cycle left a distinct signature in the thickness and extent of its sediments, their chemical composition and fossil content, the degree and nature of weathering that occurred in the intervals separating oceanic incursions. Often, sandstone was laid down first, then covered by carbonate rock, limestone or dolomite. But at times, distant geologic episodes made themselves felt; vast quantities of mud from mountain-building events that formed the

Appalachians flowed into the ancient sea and settled into layers of shale and siltstone. Some deposits were chemically converted to a sedimentary iron ore. At one point, coral reefs formed in the area of Lake Michigan.

These great inundations of water ceased about 400 million years ago, roughly the time that early terrestrial plants were evolving and vast coal swamps covered much of the eastern and central United States. A regional uplift pushed the upper Midwest above sea level; the seas retreated for the final time and left in their wake layer upon layer of sediment, thousands of feet thick, deposited over a Precambrian granitic basement. The land dried, and a long period of erosion followed, wearing away the work of oceans. Rain and wind removed hundreds of feet of rock, though not uniformly. Water drained to the low spots and, diverted by harder rock, found a path through the softer. Streams sliced channels into the land and back through time, exposing on valley floors geological strata laid down hundreds of millions of years earlier. The ridge tops weathered more slowly. Even now, a few of the very highest hills in southwest Wisconsin are capped by Silurian dolomite deposited by one of the last of the advancing oceans. Vestiges of a sheet of rock extending a thousand miles to the northeast, these hilltops were once continuous with the escarpment over which Niagara Falls still falls.

By the onset of the last glacial age 2 million years ago, much of the upper Midwest probably looked something like the driftless area does today—a well-drained land of steep hills, ridges, and rock outcrop rising between branching networks of deeply eroded watercourses. Many, perhaps most, were spring creeks rising from the porous and chemically rich aquifers formed in the depositions of ancient seas. A hundred thousand square miles of spring-creek country, it must have presented a magnificent sight and, to a trout fisherman's eye, a scarcely believable one. The glaciers rearranged nearly all of it, leaving only this driftless remnant in the heart of the heartland.

~~~~~~~~~~~

Though at some point during the last 2 million years glaciers abutted every side of the driftless area, they did not encircle it at any given time. The region was never entirely sur-rounded, an island of land rising from a sheet of continental ice. But it survives now as an island of a different sort, a 500-million-year-old landscape, a tenth the age of the earth itself, bordered by glacial country that has existed for perhaps 12,000 years, less than the blink of an eye in geologic time. It is a fragment of the past, a small piece of what once was, en-during amid the new. And though we think of glacial pro-cesses as imperceptibly gradual, the cycles of deposition and erosion that shaped the driftless area were infinitely slower, the scale of incremental change unimaginably small.

"There is a secret bond," writes Milan Kundera, "between slowness and memory, speed and forgetting." And in the long collection of sediments on the ocean floor there is a recollec-tion as well. The rock remembers and writes its history on sheets of stone, imprints it in fossils pressed like leaves in the pages of an old book, etches its story in the cursive of a spring creek inscribed on a valley floor. The land is memory and the water its remembering, breaching time to unearth the past. There is a strange first impression produced by this country, that the valleys are responsible for the streams, but it is in fact the other way around. The coulee walls, the resistant es-carpments and banks of outcrop have been stream-worn bare to the base and now rise half a billion years high. In them lies the land's memory of itself, of all the landscapes it has ever been, of Cambrian oceans and Paleozoic plateaus, layered one atop another, each mirroring the shape of the past one even as it buries it. This record is itself recorded in places named for the land—Blue Mound, Military Ridge, Hidden Valley, Timber Coulee, Cave Hollow, Spring Green.

Even the glaciers are remembered here, not in pulverized gravel and scarred rock but in the blanket of loess, a fine silt soil lifted by the wind from drying outwash plains and draped over the driftless area thirty feet thick in places. In others, north-facing bluffs have formed algific talus slopes as water percolates into the limestone and freezes; all summer long, cold air seeps from hillside vents and trickles down frost-shattered rock, pooling at the base into a cool microclimate, small fragments of an ice age that still support northern monkshood, intermediate sedge, and muskroot—plants now found much farther north that exist here as disjunct species only in a few places. And the land recalls the last glacier, the one of green that advanced from the south as vegetation reclaimed the warming, drying soil left by retreating ice. Here and there among newer immigrants, small stands of yellow birch and hemlock still hold on, the relict memories of a once vast woods that long ago moved in and then moved on, following the margin of a shrinking glacier and spreading at last into boreal forests far to the north.

Each passing life of this place has pressed some piece of itself into the land, a story told, then retold. The driftless hills are mausolea, vaulted with caves and stacked with slabs of limestone corpses, their calcified husks leached by rainwater that flows over time and trickles from springs, the mineral remains of a billion creatures cannibalized in the stream below for new shell and bone and exoskeletons. The ridge tops and plateaus are shrouded each year in fresh grass—"the beautiful, uncut hair of graves," Whitman calls it—as the living reclaim the dead. The marks of the past are still felt in the present, recalled in the trace of hills and the tracks of timeworn valleys.

The world leaves footprints deep enough in places to impress their shapes on the soul. It is no accident that we name the contours of our experience in the language of the land—we reach peaks and wage uphill fights; there are watershed events and rocky roads; we find fertile ground or make serendipitous discoveries. For there is as surely a topography to inner life as there is to what lies outside. The driftless hills are memory, and some memory is driftless, unaltered by the accumulated till of days, untouched by the glacial press of life's sheer ongoingness that cracks and grinds and reworks old stories into new ones, or carries them away. Certain places and people and times abide, the resistant outcrops of a life that are weathered into relief by a slow erosion of the delible and impermanent, laying bare the stratigraphies of a private landscape, graphed in layers of causes and consequences, bringing old stories to the light of day. They are formed to shapes of what we remember by longing, love, grief, regret, joy, and self-reproach that run like rivers and carve furrows in the heart. What remains is enduring but not immutable, for even recollection itself has a kind of friction that smooths whatever it touches, like the image on an old coin rubbed soft by constant handling. Every memory is also a forgetting, and every name an elegy.

3

Meandering

~~~~~~~~

Tell all the truth but tell it slant—

Success in Circuit lies

—Emily Dickinson

All that is gold does not glitter,

Not all those who wander are lost.

—J. R. R. Tolkien

One of the great charms of a spring creek lies in its propensity to meander, to curl roundabout through the land in looping arcs, bending first one direction, then another, sometimes doubling back on itself in a shepherd's crook so narrow that you might stand on the finger of land within and see water on either side of you flowing in opposite directions. A stream can cover a lot of territory this way, but its course is largely lateral; movement forward comes only in small increments as the current, rounding a bend, makes a little headway down the valley before turning aside once again, its onward progress—like progress of many kinds—achieved in the brief moment of changing direction. The shape alone, all crescent bank and switchback, endows the landscape with an animate quality, the flexing of a thing alive. Aside from its deep and obvious appeal to the fisherman, the geometry of meandering pleases in a purely visual sense. For the eye delights in curvatures; it is drawn to the forms of roundness and parabola, to the undulating line, to all the figures that have motion even though they stand still. The eye savors the contour of a hill or the coil of vine as the mind does a twist of plot or turn of phrase.

All running water seeks to meander, but not all conditions favor it equally. In a steep, stony riverbed, the stream is governed most immediately by the vagaries of local terrain, forced in one direction or another by the resistance of rock. In a lower gradient and in softer soils, water calls the shots. One might first and reasonably attribute the winding path of a spring creek to the simple fact that water always flows downhill, searching out the lowest point and going with the grain of the land. Meanders, then, merely reflect the subtle topography of a valley floor that may appear flat but is in reality an irregular surface of small rises and troughs, knobs and gullies that steer the stream this way and that. A spring creek is not muscular, but it is very persuasive, and in the end it is the water, not the surrounding land, that creates the meandering curves. A spring creek does not follow a course but shapes its own and so is the purest expression of the nature of moving water.

Meanders occur in the first place because no stream channel or flow of water is truly uniform. Small inconsistencies in water depth or speed, in the configuration or composition of the bottom, will inevitably alter the direction of even a perfectly straight current, causing it to strike one bank more forcefully than the other. The collision may be only slight and oblique, but that is enough. The flow of water gradually wears a hollow into the bank, and the face of this curve presents a more nearly perpendicular surface to the current and catches a greater brunt of its force, which further accelerates erosion, until finally a pronounced curve is created in the stream. The main current enters the bend, swings around its perimeter, and then keeps on going; diverted by the arc of the bend, it travels across the channel, where it strikes the opposite bank and eventually creates a second bend. Once again, the current is deflected across the streambed to the other bank, eroding yet another bend, and so on. For this reason, stream bends always occur in pairs, always on alternate sides of the stream, in more or less opposing directions; and technically speaking, the two curves taken together constitute one meander. The continuous reversals give a spring creek its characteristic, sinuous shape and create the stream structures familiar to fishermen. The faster current flowing around the outer edge of a bend digs the channel deeper, while the slower current at the inner edge allows eroded material to settle and collect. The result is a bend pool with a shallow, silty bottom on the inside shelving off to deeper, faster water on the outside—one of the most promising spots in all of angling. A pair of bend pools is separated by a stretch of straighter, shallower water, often with a riffled or broken surface; typically, the fishing is less demanding in such places, and the trout run smaller.

This two-dimensional view—a twisting line drawn on a plane—is the most visible geometry of a spring creek, but a stream actually meanders in three dimensions. Current striking a bend is not only diverted horizontally, following the curve of the bank, but is deflected slightly downward. Water hits the outside bank and curls vertically down the outside of the bend; it flows sideways across the bottom to the shallower bank, rises up to the top, and flows sideways again across the surface of the stream; in short, it circulates laterally. At the same time, of course, the water is running downstream, and the resulting combination of vectors produces a current that spirals its way through the channel. And in fact, this corkscrew effect is partly responsible for the erosional nibble at the outside of a bend and the deposition of sediments on the inside.

To fish a particular spring creek is really to fish only one of the many streams it will be in its life. For the thing about meandering is that it never stops. As long as water flows, the shape of the stream continues to change. The erosional forces that create a bend in the first place persist, cutting deeper and deeper into the outside bank while more sand and silt are deposited on the inside. As a result, the outside of the bend moves slowly away from the center of the valley, and the buildup of sediment on the inside of the bend follows along, eventually forming an exaggerated meander around a long finger of land. By this process of meandering outward, the stream widens its own valley; a bend may wander so far laterally that it touches a flanking ridge and wears away a small piece of the hillside. In time, though, the current will form two new bends that flank the finger of land like the curves in an hourglass. It's not at all uncommon when fishing a spring creek to run across such a place, an oxbow bend that doubles back on itself, nearly forming a complete circle and pinching a throat into the peninsula that may be only a few yards wide. At some point, perhaps during a high-water year or sudden flood, the stream takes a shortcut across the narrow throat of land and isolates the oxbow from any further flow of current. The stream in a sense pulls itself back toward the center of the valley; the oxbow, now literally out of the loop, becomes a stillwater slough that, in most cases, eventually dries up. If you can gain a high enough vantage point, you may see in some valleys the curved swales and arc-shaped depressions of abandoned oxbows lying on either side of the stream, the grass-covered parentheses that bracket its history.

A meandering stream alters its shape in other ways as well. Often, the current entering a bend does not strike the bank precisely at the apex of the curve, but rather at a point just downstream of the center. The force of the water erodes this area until it becomes the new center of a new arc. Sediment builds up on the inside of the bend, just downstream of the tip; the entire curve is repositioned slightly downstream, and the whole process begins over again. In this way, meanders themselves meander, gradually migrating down the valley floor, their vacated positions to be occupied in time by other bends that move in from above. Were it possible to take time-lapse photographs over a sufficiently long period, they would show the stream wriggling from side to side as it wiggles on down the valley.

But for all its apparently irregular wandering, a stream meanders with a remarkable kind of consistency. One of the most curious properties of moving water is that the shape and frequency of bends in a river are governed by the width of the channel. If you envision a meandering stream as a series of S-shaped curves—not all identical, to be sure, some symmetrical, others flattened or elongated or slightly distorted, but essentially the same figure—it turns out that the wavelength of its meander, that is the straight-line distance across any one complete S, is about eleven times the width of the stream. Moreover, the bends themselves have a radius of about two to three stream widths; all the curves are cut from pretty much the same cloth, arcs of the same circle. These relationships hold for a meandering river of any size, though no one knows precisely why they hold at all. I find it extraordinary, on the one hand, that running water configures itself not just around these specific proportions, but around proportions of any kind; at the same time, it is not altogether surprising. One comes to appreciate that interior order inheres everywhere in the natural world, patterns that ultimately have reasons—why the ratio pi, for instance, crops up so often and in such unexpected contexts, or why pigeons bob their heads when they walk—but still beg explanation.

These internal consistencies of meandering, if themselves not readily accounted for, are part of our intuitive understanding of rivers and the way in which we experience them. Fishermen, for instance, know when studying a stream on an aerial photograph or map—one with no external reference points—that it is impossible to determine if the image represents a tiny creek or a large river. Because the configuration of a channel is proportionate only to its width, their shapes are virtually identical. They differ only in scale; one is merely a miniature version of the other.

This recurrence of pattern and essential proportion sometimes produces an odd sense of familiarity when first fishing a new stream, a sense that goes beyond the obvious similarities of all moving water. It is purely a matter of curvature; whether a large river or a small one, its geometry is instinctively grasped simply because it meanders. The water above and below you, the size and number and proximity of its bends can be inferred from the water directly in front of you, how far it is from one bank to the other. All you need do is adjust the scale, and if you fish often enough, that happens pretty much without thinking. Sometimes, no adjustment at all is necessary. I was astonished to find, when I got out in the world a bit and fished the limestone creeks of Pennsylvania, the small chalkstreams of England, and the spring creeks of the West, how closely they resembled waters I knew in the driftless area. The similarity had less to do with the simple fact that they were all small creeks and everything to do with the identical forms of meandering that this smallness produced—the same compactness of the oxbows, the length of glides and runs, the frequency of bends and placement of undercuts. I instantly understood their proportions, and if in the end this did not help a great deal in the matter of catching fish, it certainly increased the pleasure of being there. Spring creeks are among the most treasured waters in trout fishing, and the familiar geometry of meandering may be one of the reasons.

A meandering stream takes the shape it must, conforming to the principles of dynamics and work and energy balance. But as in other forms that shape themselves around other constraints—the hexagon of snowflakes or the helix of DNA, a sonnet or the blues—the borders still afford ample room for variety and distinctiveness. A few basic ratios of arithmetic can give rise to the most elegant improvisations. A spring creek meanders through shapely permutations, through close, backtracking turns that nearly touch one another; in regular, rhythmic alternations, clean as a sine wave; around right-angle corners; along flexing arcs that wobble as they bend; and through the graceful, elongated S-curves that are perhaps the loveliest of all. The eighteenth-century painter William Hogarth called this curve "the line of beauty" and pronounced it the most aesthetically perfect of all shapes. It is a line of both motion and repose, a figure repeated in the dip and swell of rolling hills, the swerve of schooling fish, the twist of a vine through the understory, the curve of a woman's back. In a painting, Hogarth said, this line of beauty "leads the eye on a wanton kind of chase." In nature, it leads the feet as well.

Meandering is the curve of curiosity and exploration and sometimes of discovery—digressive and indirect, obedient only to an inner logic of its own but open to serendipity, its own justification because it answers to something elemental in nature, human and otherwise. Now here, now there, a meander is the tack of interesting conversation, the turn of unhurried musing, the unpremeditated detours of an aimless walk, the afternoon circuit of a well-fed dog with no appointments. Meandering is the shape of youth with time on its hands, when the years are still a given, life's automatic entitlement, and the hours not yet a currency to be saved and invested and spent in the calculus of cost/benefit, with an eye toward economy and value. Later, when life gains velocity and assumes a more predictable trajectory, meandering grows more difficult. While a few still manage it, most of us are driven to simulate it in peculiar oxymoronic behaviors—planning for unplanned time, forcing ourselves to relax, running to stand still. But in those years before the present becomes enslaved to some ever receding future, one is blissfully unshackled from the value of things—of a dollar or a day—and things are free to acquire their own value. All time is now, and a day merely the meandering arc of moments laid end to end. Sometimes, youth does indeed seem wasted on the young. Then again, it's all they really have.

It was in just such a wandering and indirect fashion that I came to know the driftless area and its spring creeks. Finding trout was the end but meandering the means, and even now I can scarcely imagine country better suited to this wanton kind of chase. Nothing is so tempting as a geography of small concealments, all nook and hollow and shady bend, every stream a line of beauty on the valley floor, every one-lane blacktop disappearing into the hills begging to be followed just to see where it leads.

Almost always, a small group of us set out, brothers and friends and brothers of friends, the precise number and makeup shifting from trip to trip, depending on who was around, who would make good company, who could be trusted to appreciate whatever small discoveries might be made. Informal and unstructured, it was less an expeditionary force than a fishing version of pickup basketball. A few us made every trip and so became a kind of de facto core, though to call us "leaders" would imply a level of organization hilariously beyond the facts. We were merely the guys who brought the ball. Regardless of the specific participants, however, our aggregate angling qualifications amounted to little more than a fishing rod apiece and unremitting optimism, and over the course of many summers, we burned an unholy amount of time knocking around the countryside, fishing and exploring.

One of our first discoveries was that there were two routes to almost every trout stream. The quick way was the most linear course with the fastest roads; not necessarily a short trip in absolute terms, its degree of quickness was relative to the second approach, the back way. Almost always, we took the back way, zigzagging through a checkerboard of cornfields, alternately west and north, entering the driftless area from the south, where it dipped a short distance into Illinois. For a carload of amped-up fishermen wired to be on the water, it seems an odd choice, I suppose, this circuitous traveling that made a drive of two hours into something more like three. "More scenic," we agreed, though we passed through it before daylight. No one ever publicly pointed out this discrepancy, privately relishing instead the sense of a sidelong route to a secret place, of somehow sneaking in undetected beneath the world's radar—a small thrill, to be sure, but along with the cool midwestern night streaming in through the car window, enough to raise the hair on my arms every time.

We generally stopped twice along the back way, first briefly in a small, trim farming town—call it Dutch Cove—that marked the entrance to trout country. In a tiny seizure of civic pride, the inhabitants had constructed a little monument of sorts, a concrete pedestal off the side of the road on which was mounted a half-scale Liberty-type bell. An explanatory bronze plaque commemorating the specific occasion was screwed to the side, but there was never enough light to read it. We eased up slowly, headlights off; one of us would spring from the idling car, give the clapper a mighty heave, and bolt back inside, speeding off as a single, thundering peal reverberated through the silent streets. We did this every time. It's what passed for "tradition" in those days. We had nothing at all against the good folks of Dutch Cove, just a certain irresistible overflow of animal spirits. And if I felt a twinge of guilt, I also figured that the townspeople were probably used to it and perhaps deserved to regret their error: take a device expressly constructed to make noise, leave it fully functional and unguarded fifteen feet from the main road, and what else can you realistically expect? Any rational community planning board, no matter how small, should contain at least one sixteen-year-old boy.

Not many miles down the road, we stopped again, this time for gas at the suitably named Holiday Service Station, since by this point in the trip, beyond the halfway mark, a certain carnival-like atmosphere prevailed in the car. Holiday was one link in a once thriving chain of establishments that have since gone belly-up, the sad fate of so many enterprises ahead of their time. For in Holiday, one beheld the gas station of the future. It had no service bays, no racks of wiper blades and quart oil cans, no stacks of tires, no pump jockeys. In place of all this was a gleaming market of the type that would come to be known as a "convenience store" and eventually scatter its spawn along every stretch of asphalt in

America. Holiday was a primitive but recognizable version, a kind of ur-Mini-Mart, a proto-Kwik-Stop where you could procure virtually everything except, in one of its most enduring legacies, service for your car. But it was pure retail lodestone, and after gassing up we swarmed inside to buy soft drinks, junk food, and other requisite teenage fuels.

This proved, however, no ordinary transaction. The minds behind the whole Holiday concept had devised as well a promotional scheme to lure and keep any customers still leery of this visionary idea. At the conclusion of a purchase, the cashier doled out, along with any change you had coming, a certain quantity of Bonus Bucks, the precise number calculated as a fraction of the original sale. Bonus Bucks functioned as a kind of in-house Monopoly money, a private scrip redeemable only within the confines of Holiday, but good as cash there. From the first, I was much taken with the resourceful, free-enterprise swagger of this idea—print your own money: it was so thoroughly American. So we gathered up our Bonus Bucks, wandered back through the aisles, and beneath buzzing banks of fluorescent tubes, hunted for what might be had.

Like all conceptions of deep genius, though, this one had its flaw. Having brought this second round of selections to the checkout stand and surrendered our Bonus Bucks, we received in return . . . more Bonus Bucks! . . . albeit a smaller number, but still enough to suck us into the gaping Holiday vortex, an ever diminishing consumer feedback loop in which every purchase earns a premium, which in turn demands a new purchase. Acquiring what you needed, or even wanted, ceased to have any meaning, and the sole objective became exhausting the supply of Bonus Bucks—that is to say, buying for its own sake, which is another thoroughly American idea. As the number of Bonus Bucks diminished with each repetition of the cycle, the quantity and type of merchandise within their reach shrank correspondingly, and our purchases grew ever smaller and more useless, until the cashier finally bagged the pitiful last of it—a foil packet of Bromo-Seltzer, a few souvenir pencils, a key ring from which dangled the plastic head of Vince Lombardi.

Once I tried to short-circuit the whole Bonus Bucks phenomenon by suggesting to a young woman at the cash register that she envision it not as a series of discrete transactions but as a self-contained microeconomic system that occupied a sort of simultaneous present. I bought, as I remember, something like ten dollars' worth of gasoline and provisions. We both know, I told her, that I'll be receiving, say, two Bonus Bucks for my patronage. Instead of pointlessly shuffling them back and forth between us, why not just apply them now as a credit against my bill? I now owe eight dollars. In a moment, I will pay it and earn about another dollar and a half in Bonus Bucks. Since these are essentially mine already, let's just use them now to reduce the total to $6.50. It was early in the morning, and if she wasn't exactly persuaded, she was becoming sufficiently bewildered, and had I stopped there, I might have pulled it off. But I got a little too caught up in trying to out-Holiday the Holiday system and continued pushing this advance-retroactive-payment idea through successive iterations until the tab was almost zero. I don't believe she ever quite figured out what was happening, and certainly never saw the beauty of it, but in the end she refused to make the paradigm leap.

The Holiday experience always proved as surreal as the place itself, which I remember chiefly as a hemisphere of light glowing against a black background—the white-enameled building, the chrome pumps, the jaunty futuristic logo suspended from its curved support all sparkled in the bluish-purple illumination of a dozen mercury-vapor lamps like some bizarre extraterrestrial landing site.

I never saw the place in daytime. Our trips invariably began so early in the morning that it was functionally the dead of night. I remained inflexible on this point, convinced, in the first place, that trout fishing was always best at dawn (it almost always wasn't) and, in the second, that some virtuousness attached to the wee hours, that a little suffering merited reward, that if we didn't actually catch fish, we at least deserved to. Half of an angling life is built of such groundless absurdities, and the other half of one's inflexible belief in them. I'm not sure if my companions shared these precise convictions, but they were game enough, and we resolved to be on the water by first light. Sometimes, though, we hit a pothole on the road from intention to outcome, and things did not always go according to plan. Like the Bonus Bucks, the human system is a marvel of flawed engineering. Its instruments of internal regulation, the chemical sensors and governors, the hormonal gyroscopes are calibrated to keep things purring under the operating conditions of daily life. But in extreme circumstances, endocrine overdose and supersaturated neurotransmitters can bring about peculiar, paradoxical malfunctions. People cry out of sheer joy or perform the most daring acts of courage when they are most terrified. In our case, underrested from a short night's sleep, overstimulated by the prospect of fishing, and accelerated by sugar-and-salt afterburners, we'd arrive streamside right on schedule and promptly crash into a postadrenaline coma, not waking until the day was already hours old. At once, four car doors would blow open and five or six bodies spill out en masse, dash to the tailgate and burrow into a great congestion of gear, disentangling rods, sorting out creels, jackets, and shoes from empty pop cans and crumpled cellophane bags, then scramble to the stream in a scene of chaos that generally resembled the fall of Saigon, but without the helicopters.

But this was only sometimes. Normally, we had little trouble remaining conscious and controlled our impatience long enough to rig up in the half-light of dawn. For a time, we used only spinning tackle, and among us managed an assortment of rods and reels so miscellaneous that in the end they shared only one common characteristic—a complete ill-fittedness for small-stream trout fishing. In this regard, they bore striking resemblance to their users and so suited us rather well. Beyond rod and reel, each of us was outfitted according to his own idiosyncratic notions, though on the whole we tried to keep it simple. No one wore waders or a vest or carried a net or lugged around extra baggage of any kind. Fishing small streams requires keeping on the move, and anything beyond the bare basics only proves an encumbrance in the long haul. We typically, if presumptuously, slung a canvas creel over one shoulder. A little container of #14 gold Aberdeen hooks, split shot, and a few tiny spinners went into one shirt pocket. Worms went into the other. We discovered that a little bedding or loamy soil in a pocket and frequent sprinklings with water for evaporation cooling sufficed as a morning's life-support system for half a dozen nightcrawlers. And if it didn't, you could tell pretty easily when things were heading south. A troubled worm begins to smell even before it turns toes up; then it passes briefly through the corpse stage and in remarkably short time simply disintegrates without a trace. This was another thing we discovered: that worms are really little more than a loosely organized and slightly mobile form of dirt.

Though crudely appointed, we were hardly the freckled-faced apparitions from some Norman Rockwell hallucination, an image we despised as the cloying and fatuous fabrication of a man who had most certainly never fished, the whole ethos of its bent safety pin an insult to anglers everywhere. We were out to have fun, of course, but our fun was a great deal different from mere frivolousness. It was a more serious kind of fun, fun with a little weight to it. On the other hand, we were a long way from that other, solemn creature, the stream technician, who fishes with the joyless deportment of a man who must chair a summit conference right after he performs brain surgery. Our fishing neither lark nor labor, our gear only minimal and approximate, we were more like trout fishing's version of a recently paroled inmate, with his too tight shoes, thirty-dollar suit, and bus fare—underequipped but overjoyed, and hardly complaining.

In this humor, we struck out across the meadows, singly or in pairs, to favorite bends or stretches, hiking through the waist-high, dewy grasses and drenched to the skin by the time we reached water. In early mornings, the particular water was most likely to be a stream I will call Jerusalem Creek—the very one recorded in the journal kept by Hawker's grandfather, the place where I caught my first trout, the same stream that in a few years I would fish again and again in my imagination. Beginning at Jerusalem Creek was also one of our traditions, which is another way of saying that it was a cyclic, self-reinforcing behavior. We fished here first because we caught trout, and we caught trout because we knew it best, and we knew it best because we fished here first—applying the same kind of circular question begging that passes for logic in most of what trout fishermen do. In this respect we were off to a good start.

Jerusalem Creek is a fairly typical driftless-area spring creek. It heads near the juncture of two ridges where they meet to form a V and meanders more or less north through the small valley between, as the ridges gradually diverge to the east and west. A winding asphalt road parallels the stream for most of its length—a distance of perhaps six or seven miles—though the road takes its own meander, sometimes veering away from the water half a mile or more, some-

times approaching within a few yards, though actually cross-
ing the stream only twice. In its upper three miles, Jerusalem
Creek flows in a narrow channel over a shallow, sandy bottom, and though a few trout doubtless hang out there, it is
small, murderous to fish, and generally unpromising. I tried
hiking this stretch once, hoping to find a few deeper pools or
bends. There would not be many, but it was unlikely that
anyone had fished them, and spring-creek trout, undisturbed
in an out-of-the-way place, can grow very large. But I found
nothing and gave it up after a mile or so. Below this point, the
creek veers away from the road in a wide loop and somewhere along the way gains volume, perhaps from springs
where the channel brushes the base of the western ridge, for
when it circles back into view, the creek, though still small,
carries noticeably more water and looks like a real trout
stream.

The valley, too, grows wider here, technically wide
enough to till, though the meandering creek carves the bottomland into plots that are mostly too small and irregular for
cultivation. Here and there, a little ribbon of land, a single
tractor pass in width, might be planted in corn or oats; somewhat more is in pasture, but most of it is simply left to run
wild in red, yellow, and white clover; milkweed; goldenrod;
fleabane and black-eyed Susans; Queen Anne's lace; chickory
and vetch; mullein, campion, and dock; wild mustard; hawk-
weed; yarrow and toadflax; a dozen species of grass and
dozens more of other plants. Fencerows of rusted three-string
barbed wire cross-hatch the land in places, drawing boundaries that no longer correspond to any existing pattern of use,
their meaning now only a memory. The lower three miles or
so of Jerusalem Creek course through this patchwork of
fields, pastures, and overgrown meadows, and this was our
territory.

These few miles, I suppose, were an absurdly short stretch of water, especially on a small stream, over which to have lavished so many summer mornings, the kind of thing that would soon exhaust its appeal for more seasoned fishermen. But there is no necessary correspondence between how big a place is and how big it feels. If our stretch of Jerusalem Creek was small, our experience of it was large, in part because we were inexperienced. We learned the stream by learning to fish it and learned how to fish by learning the stream, in a haphazardly reciprocal form of self-instruction. The increments of this education, particularly as measured in trout, were small, but each gain became a kind of lens that enlarged the place. A minor skill mastered, a fresh idea, a dawning possibility—all of these give a fisherman new eyes, and new eyes see a new stream. We might stumble upon trout in a type of water we always bypassed as inferior, or we might venture some refinement in tackle that suddenly allowed us to fish places previously beyond our methods. Such discoveries transformed a familiar stream into unexplored territory, a whole creek's worth of water we hadn't fished or hadn't fished in a particular way. Or we might have a streak of good luck and return the next time not with any new knowledge or skill but only with greater confidence, a heightened sense of the possible that was enough to make Jerusalem Creek into a brand-new place. On each trip, we found a different stream because, each time, the place made us different fishermen, if not necessarily better ones. We'd try this idea or that technique, sometimes based on observation or reasonable surmise but more often on flawed assumptions, on coincidence masquerading as pattern, on groundless speculation. It scarcely mattered. Each idea or approach, erroneous or otherwise, became a kind of wedge that opened up the landscape a little and showed it in a different light. In the

end, we came to know the place by the same sidelong, looping indirection by which the stream knows its own valley.
We crossed and recrossed the small, familiar terrain of
Jerusalem Creek countless times, yet it never lost its capacity for surprise, and that made the place large, and still does.

There was room enough in any case to have a stretch of
stream to yourself, though we never divided up the water in
any formal way and frequently ended up running across one
another during a morning's fishing. Small creeks don't offer
many places where you can park yourself and work a spot for
a couple of hours, as you might on a big river. You tend to
keep moving, and with five or six of us out there somewhere,
it was almost inevitable that we would cross paths, sometimes passing with just a wave, sometimes stopping to fish
together, sharing the water by leapfrogging bends. Perhaps
because my early tastes were formed along these lines, I still
value above all the kind of fishing day that passes in the alternating rhythm of being alone and being in company. Both
solitude and society are improved on a trout stream. Of fishing in private, there's little enough to say—it is one of life's
dearest enjoyments. But there is pleasure too in catching up
with a partner from time to time and checking in just to see
how it's going. And if the fishing is slow, a casual exchange
can easily turn into a long conversation, which is another
thing I like about it. If one of us happened to find an excep-
tionally good spot, which is to say more than one trout was
actually caught there, he quickly summoned his nearest
companion, since hogging such bounty was unthinkable. So
while we focused, as fishermen must, on keeping our lines
wet, there was also a certain amount of coming and going, of
wandering up and down the stream looking for good water. It
was a thoroughly and happily disorganized affair, and I've always imagined that viewed from a height, our movements
had a certain antlike quality to them, the stoppings and start-

ings and brief touching of antennae, each individual creature moving with at least distantly discernible purpose, while any logic of their collective activity remained a mystery.

We went at it steadily and hard for most of the morning, even when our efforts met with the indifference that is so often the fate of the righteous. As midday neared, however, we might stash our rods for a while and just amble through a meadow hunting out interesting plants or insects, or hike up the rocky bluff that overlooked the valley, or peck away with a rock hammer at great blocks of limestone, looking for fossils. Or we might catch a nap, flaking out on the streamside grass or dozing in the car, feet protruding from an open door. But by noon, the last of us would straggle back from wherever, and we would trade our various accounts of the morning, produce what trout we'd caught for general admiration, eat lunch if we'd remembered to bring it, and ponder a change of venue.

Jerusalem Creek, we believed—rightly in the beginning, wrongly in later years—gave us our best shot at catching fish, and so as I have said it became the customary early-morning starting point. But it was also a point of departure for afternoons spent driving around the countryside looking for new trout streams. Although we referred to these rambles as "scouting," the term suggests a more purposeful and workmanlike quality than they actually possessed; they were part fishing, part just looking around, part pure joyride. These ventures began with no agenda and followed no itinerary, but they were not altogether random either. What loose direction we had came from a small booklet entitled, as I recall, *Wisconsin Trout Streams* and assembled by the Department of Natural Resources. I obtained the book through a vigorous campaign of letter writing to every state agency that might have some information about trout fishing, or might know where to acquire it, or might know someone who might know how to get it. It was the first guidebook to trout streams that I'd ever seen and the first of dozens that I would accumulate over the years, but certainly a crude one compared to its modern counterpart. The contemporary destination book is a wonder of specificity and thoroughness, putting you on good water with almost frightening efficiency, yet at the same time sapping some of the mystery and adventure from finding new places. *Wisconsin Trout Streams*, however, posed no threat in either of these regards and bore about the same resemblance to the modern where-to guide as the Lascaux Caves to the Louvre. Its crudeness stemmed in part from a genre still in its infancy and in part from its authorship—a collection of low-level government functionaries, none of whom, I am certain, fished. When I first saw the book, it was already twenty-five years old, about the same vintage, I calculated, as the journal kept by Hawker's grandfather, and I wondered if that old man had seen or used it and thought he probably had.

The authors of this booklet dutifully sectioned the state into quadrants and the quadrants into counties and for each county listed the names of waters that met some unspecified DNR criteria for a Wisconsin trout stream. The species of trout in each of the waters was identified, and each stream classified according to whether these trout were wild, stocked, or a combination of the two. On simple pen-and-ink outline maps of the quadrants, each stream was drawn in, each meandering line so distinctive (and ultimately so accurate) as to leave no doubt that it had been scrupulously reproduced from a detailed topographical map. But in the end, the booklet was a government document and so embodied the bureaucrat's unerring instinct to mismatch form and function, to fret endlessly over minor details while somehow remaining blind to the big picture. Painstaking as they were in their replication of each stream, the maps contained no towns or highways or backroads or natural landmarks or reference points of any kind. In short, they consisted of big, empty white spaces with little creeks scribbled inside, and nothing more, as though the primary concern was this indisputable record of a trout stream's existence, while actually being able to find the place was a matter of no conceivable relevance.

To locate one of these streams required a second set of maps and great patience—marking its position relative to quadrant borders in the booklet and searching on a big county map for a stream of the corresponding shape. In a landscape riven with small creeks, this was far more difficult than it sounds. The names of streams did not prove a reliable guide, and for the most part we identified possible waters through the process of elimination, guesswork, and hunch. But in its way, the booklet suited us perfectly; it was as primitive and partial a guidebook as we were fishermen. More suggestive than definitive, long on pointing but short on actual direction, obsessed with irrelevant detail, deficient in all vital particulars except the tantalizing names of unknown trout streams, it was the ideal handbook for meandering. We did not follow it because it did not lead; it only gestured vaguely, and we took off from there. Had we possessed back then a modern fishing guide to the driftless area—of which there are now several—we would have found more fish in less time, but I doubt we would have come to know the place a tenth as well.

So after lathering up Jerusalem Creek in the morning, we spent afternoons riding to the hounds of possibility, chasing down conjectures circled on a sheaf of foxed and dog-eared maps, doing more looking than finding, more traveling than fishing. Some of the officially sanctioned streams had apparently seen better days, for we worked a few of them several times and never saw a single trout or sign of one. Then again, we found unlisted streams that held fish, and these were highly prized. But as a rule, we never knew quite where we were, if we had correctly translated the uncontextualized booklet maps into navigable destinations, whether we were indeed fishing a "Wisconsin trout stream" or something else. Not that we cared much, for we were always somewhere, on the water or on the road to water, and the specifics, while a matter of interest, were of no great importance. We were looking for trout streams, not really any stream in particular, and in this respect one was as good as another. Our enthusiasm for this sort of thing never flagged. The dead ends and disappointments were numerous but short-lived, always eclipsed by anticipation of the next place, for if you choose to wander about, scouting anything, you might as well do it with high expectations; to meander without hope is a pitiable spectacle and a fool's errand.

In any exploration involving trout, bridges acquire an almost mystical significance, giving both a vantage point from which to assess the likeliness of new water and a point of access should it appear plausible. To crest a hill and spot a bridge in the distance was always a moment of high excitement. We would drive over it slowly, six heads swiveling in unison as they sized up the water, asking the same question, applying a taxonomy that possessed but two categories: a) trout stream, and b) not. This kind of determination is hard to make just by looking, so if there was water at all, we almost always ended up wetting a line, and as a result we fished some truly dreadful places—turbid, swampy ditches; streams that cut low tunnels through impossible thickets; little creeks carrying no more flow than a garden hose. We might have been more discriminating, but we sometimes caught trout in these unpromising places and so became cautious about dismissing even the most improbable water. When you got right down to it, we would fish almost anywhere, pulling off at a bridge, piling out of the car, and spreading along the banks of some sluggish mudhole, plying it with our best moves. From time to time, some farmer high in the seat of his John Deere would stop in midfield, engine idling, and watch us for a while in . . . amusement? disbelief? nostalgia? It was hard to tell at that distance.

Whether or not it proved to be a trout stream depended entirely on whether or not we caught trout, and even we knew that our abilities in this regard were a monumentally imprecise yardstick with which to measure anything. Then, too, from the standpoint of catching fish, these afternoon scouting ventures had a certain built-in, self-defeating quality, since we always set out for new water at the very worst time of day, when the sun was high and hot. We fished some beautiful places with no results, but we also found trout streams and some jewels among them—Emerald Creek, Hummingbird Branch, Mariposa Creek, Redstone Brook— places that would supplant Jerusalem Creek as most favored water when, in time, we began fly fishing. Discovering a new trout stream is a wonderful thing, and even if its whereabouts are common knowledge, to come upon the place yourself for the first time is nonetheless true discovery. One by one, I logged these finds on a map in my mind, each one glowing like an ember warm with promise, a threshold of some indefinable kind. The other, troutless, streams might prove to be lovely water or make a pretty drive, but in the end they lacked the central secret at their heart. And I thought of these places as cold fires, streams that must have once shimmered with trout but had somehow died out.

When our scouting was done for the day, if there was time, we hauled out the maps and plotted a homeward course that took us past still other creeks—not to fish, just to stand on the bridge and look and to wander back on a route never taken before.

In this roundabout way, our understanding of Jerusalem Creek grew a little deeper, a little more subtle, a little fuller, and as we crisscrossed the driftless area looking for trout, our experience of the landscape became wider and more inclusive, though we explored only a fraction of this place that held a lifetime's worth of water. Each spring creek taught us something new, and we carried that idea back to other places, and so each stream was remade each time we fished it, increasingly familiar but always brand-new. Such backtracking, piecemeal approaches are not the quick way but are perhaps the most authentic. Indirection, I think, is the path of all intimate knowing. It is the way you come to learn both the places and people closest to the heart. You find them out gradually and in fragments—in flashes of personality, in quiet glimpses of character, in fleeting moods, in bits of biography, and even in those elusive parts that you will never come to understand—and you patch these together into a story you tell yourself that is all about why you love them.

We learned too, and in a similarly unsystematic fashion, how to fish a trout stream, acquiring the bulk of our education through trial and error—an expression, I might point out, of exquisite precision, since the term carries with it not the slightest whiff of success, only a sequence of efforts and mistakes. Its principal effect is not so much learning how to do something right as how to avoid making the same mistake the next time. And as a method of instruction, this one reinvents a lot of wheels and takes the long way around, eliminating all possible errors until what remains is more or less correct. But it is also how the thing often goes, this paring away to converge on some core of the workable and proof, were any needed, that there is as much meaning in loss as there is in gain.

This is how I view the matter now, of course, looking back at it through a telescope with a thirty-three-year magnification. But at the time, there was just catching trout or not catching them. We never considered ourselves as "learning" to fish, and put to us that way, we would have found the idea laughable. We weren't learning to fish; we were fishing—wholly occupied by the thing itself, never considering ourselves at all. And perhaps this is why it all took root and grew in us, not because we thought about it, but because we didn't. Later in life, setting out consciously to master something involves a kind of detachment from it. But youth is fully engaged precisely because it is unreflective. There is no distinction between learning and doing; the word "practice" has not yet divided itself into the opposed meanings of "rehearsal" and "performance," and the world is not yet a place where "practicing" the banjo and "practicing" medicine both make sense. And this, more than a long future, or the luxury of idealism, or great expectations, is the most enviable commodity of youth—the way in which life is as simply and thoughtlessly absorbed as oxygen.

In a world that for some mad purpose is hell-bent on patterning all human endeavor on the "business model," one hears much from psychologists, production engineers, education-school types, and other true believers about the "learning curve." They speak of it with earnestness and devotion, and if you are not careful, they will force their simple-hearted diagrams upon you and explain the smooth, cleanly rising line of achievement, the continuously compounded interest on human capital. You can only smile and nod politely, because telling them the truth would be too cruel, too dispiriting. For the curve of learning is a meander, the shape of a spring creek on a valley floor, given its own interior consistency by curiosity and desire and a sense of the beautiful. With a lot of traveling sideways to gain a little distance forward, with more motion than progress, it's not terribly efficient but in the end covers the ground pretty well.

Tracing and retracing the same territory inscribes a pattern on the mind, a map etched by synaptic charge and the flow of electrons through neurochemical conduits. The brain itself is ridged and furrowed like a watershed, because current everywhere behaves the same. It is a topography so distinct and durable that, far into senescence, it is sometimes all that remains, a landscape through which to wander a second time, an equivocal compensation and a strange kind of mercy.

4

Objects in Mirror Are Closer Than They Appear

~~~~~~~~

When we discover how long it takes for the atoms of the brain

to be replaced by other atoms, we come to realize that the thing

I call my individuality is only a pattern or dance. The atoms

come into my brain, dance a dance, and then go out, always

new atoms but always performing the same dance,

remembering what the dance was yesterday.

—Richard P. Feynman, *The Pleasure of Finding Things Out*

The historical origins of fly fishing are almost certainly irretrievable. Even the earliest mentions of angling with an artificial fly—which, one would imagine, come long after the actual beginnings—are meager and brief. A few lines here place the source in Macedonia, a few lines there place it in China, and in either case you are left with only a general geographical location and vague reference to some device employing feathers or wool, but no hint at all of how the thing might have been used. Against a backdrop of nothing, speculation abounds. My private theory is that the first, faint spark of fly fishing was ignited when ancient man one day noticed that a floating feather, perhaps molted from some waterfowl, occasionally lured a trout from hiding and drew it to the surface for a quick inspection. Back at the hut, he gathered a handful of feathers plucked from last night's grouse, returned to the river, and cast them on the water; when a fish rose up to take a look, our man drove a spear through its side. This is, of course, just conjecture; the only substantiation I can offer is that, first, our most cherished traditions generally have rude and unsentimental beginnings; possession, even if it is only symbolic, lurks deep in the heart of every angler, or at least those who are any good at it. And second, I just don't think of ancient man as being in much of a humor to fool around.

The origins of what might be called "modern" fly fishing, however—that is, the combination of practices, ideas, and attitudes that more or less prevail today—are easier to pin down, since they date back little more than a century or so. Without gross injustice to the historical record, we can trace the source back to the English angler Frederic Halford, who was the first, perhaps most meticulous, and certainly most zealous proponent of the notions that inform fly angling today—that is, fishing a) with the dry fly, b) upstream, c) on a drag-free float, and d) to rising or visible trout. He might also be credited with advocating, though less strenuously, two other principles that are inseparable from modern trout fishing—hatch matching and an attentiveness to stream entomology—though the most articulate spokesmen for these ideas would come along a bit later. (One is tempted to add to the list of Halford's legacies a certain style of address still widespread among self-proclaimed angling kahunas—a tone that is by turns bullying, patronizing, exasperated, and flippantly dismissive of dissenting opinion—but this manner doubtless predates Halford by millennia.) Halford himself did not devise any of these angling ideas; they were developed and practiced, though more or less independently of one another, decades or even centuries before he came on the scene. His contribution was to draw them together and systematize them into a kind of fly-fishing code or canon and, from the pulpit of several books, to preach, cajole, shame, exhort, and otherwise bludgeon most of the known trout-fishing world into conformity with his dogma. Halford was to modern fly fishing what the Four Evangelists were to Christianity—less the inventors than the architects of a religion. He regarded his convictions as more than just a means to successful fishing; they were allied with an idea of sportsmanship and a sporting life, civilized stream demeanor, and ethical practice, and his inflexible insistence upon them indeed had a moral fervor about it.

To get some idea of the extent to which Halford's brand of dry-fly purism suffused the sport, one need only take a look at his chief antagonist, G. E. M. Skues, who came along a few years later and is arguably second only to Halford in influencing the shape of the modern angling imagination. What Halford had done for the dry fly, Skues did for the artificial nymph. Halford would have none of it, and so commenced one of the legendary battles in fly fishing—dry fly versus nymph—and one that persists, though in a diminished form, into our time. The quarrel was surprisingly heated given the tiny stakes, but what is more surprising still is that the two men in fact disagreed about very little. Skues endorsed nearly all of Halford's premises, and even his most famous work championing the use of nymphs bears the distinctly beta-dog title *Minor Tactics of the Chalk Stream.* Except for the choice of fly style—a significant difference in one respect but also, in the overall set of angling ideas they advocated, probably the least important—they pretty much saw eye to eye on imitative fly patterns based on the observation of natural insects, presented upstream, dead-drift, to visible trout. It is testimony to the dominance of Halford's ideas that, first, Skues embraced almost all of them, and second, one small deviation could cause such a ruckus. And Halford's basic formulation of the sport (supplemented by Skues's contribution if you wish) is still the principal current that runs through fly fishing today.

This is not to say that everyone, or many people at all, fish like Halford or Skues. It is worth pointing out, however, that even the contemporary fly-fishing heretics routinely pilloried by the remnant strain of purism in the sport—those who fish salmon-egg imitations, or use bobberlike strike indicators, or fish nymphs so heavily weighted they deserve their own atomic numbers—still tend to fish upstream on a dead drift and subscribe to at least some loose theory of imitative fly patterns. But the way in which Halford defined the sport endures even more as an idea about fly fishing than as a set of practices; though it is evident to some degree in the way people fish, it is even more so in the way they prefer to fish, and most apparent of all in the way they say they prefer to fish. The dominance is conceptual. Halford's brand of dry-fly purism may not embrace many anglers these days, but it has a firm hold on the imaginations of nearly of all them. Upstream-dry-fly-rising-trout fishing is still envisioned as the defining idea of the sport, its most difficult or sophisticated or purest form, somehow the "best" way to fish, even among people who don't do it. It has the status of myth. The evidence is everywhere—in advertising, in biases of tackle and fly design, in the favored angling destinations. Consider that most durable icon in all of angling literature, the tweeded, pipe-smoking, bamboo-wielding purist—a creature, I suspect, that existed (if he existed at all in America) in numbers so small that he was functionally apocryphal. He is an instantly recognizable archetype, both a legacy of the Halford tradition and a vehicle of its transmission. And though these days he is most often trotted out to make sport of, it is his very familiarity, the automatic recognition of what he stands for, that makes him possible as a figure of satire at all. Or take American angling's somewhat derivative contribution to Halford, Vince Marinaro's *A Modern Dry-Fly Code*. This rather imperious title scarcely raises an eyebrow. Yet if a long-lost companion volume suddenly came to light—say, *A Modern Streamer Code*—it would be good for a few laughs at the bar. No one would take such a thing seriously.

Halford and Skues did not develop their ideas over whiskey and cigars in a chair at the club. They worked out their approaches, refined their principles, experimented, and defined their ideas on the English chalkstreams, for the simple reason that that is where they fished. Their methods, even philosophies, could not help but reflect the particular demands and attributes of these waters and their trout. Stealth, the precise presentation and natural behavior of the fly, and fishing upstream from the position of greatest concealment are virtues on any stream, of course, but nowhere more essential than on insect-rich waters full of cautious, well-fed trout. Even the ethical twist in their ideas, that the responsible sportsman does not fish the water but casts only to visible trout, can be traced in part to the placid, clear, well-manicured waters that make it possible to see fish at all. Had they honed their craft in the Scottish Highlands, for instance, it is doubtful that this stricture would have become part of the program. To the extent, then, that Halford and Skues shaped the modern angling imagination, modern fly fishing, partly as practice but even more as an idea, was born on spring creeks and grew from the particular character of these unusual waters.

I fished a long time without knowing any of this, but I wasn't at all surprised when I found it out. There had always seemed to me a certain compatibility between fly fishing and spring creeks, by which I mean first and always the streams of driftless country. And even after I had fished more widely, no water and no landscape felt as though it matched the method quite so well. Both, as I've suggested, are superbly visual. Although many waters run clear, and many others flow with glassy, unruffled currents, and still others support a lush aquatic vegetation, a spring creek blends these attributes in the most appealing harmonies of color, texture, and transparency. No other type of water better pleases the eye. A spring creek is the most visually engaging of all trout streams and fly fishing the most visually engaging of all methods. Their shapes mirror one another; the arc of a rod, the curl of a cast, the snake of a drifting line reproduce in miniature the meandering water, the roll of hilltops against the horizon, the sweep of a slope to the valley floor. It is all contour and fluid curve.

The driftless area, like the English chalkstreams and indeed like a great many spring-creek landscapes, has a kind of gentleness about it. A pastoral place of small farms nestled in hollows between wooded hills, the countryside is settled but not settled out of existence, a compromise of sorts between the civilized and the wild that gives the land an intimate, domestic quality. I have no doubt that the first fly fisherman, sitting before the hearth, fashioned the first flies from the materials of this same domesticity—from ram's wool and cock feathers, horsehair and beeswax. The tying of flies and fishing them and the landscape itself all share the same mesmerizing quality of looking into a fire. A trout fly recalls the land in the way of all handmade things, and a fishing vest is nothing if not a small household that we carry with us into the field.

Like a spring creek, fly fishing is a quiet space, more nearly paced to the rhythm of reflection than of drama. As a result, I am baffled by the recent spate of media images that attempt to portray fly fishing as an "extreme sport," a place for loonies on the edge, another drug for the thrill junkie, a test of physical and psychological limits for those with a death wish. I saw a magazine advertisement recently (pushing fly rods, I believe) that is not atypical: a well-muscled Calvin Klein boy toy up to his armpits in a foaming river, his body angled outrageously into a sweeping current, rivulets of water pouring from his jacket sleeves and streaming from his hooded visage, big coils of running line clenched in his grimacing teeth, arms poised at the fulcrum of a Herculean double-haul—and all of this viewed indistinctly through a screen of driving snow. I'm no fair-weather fisherman, but I find these man-versus-river images perfectly incredible. Just what part of this is supposed to look like fun? I suppose such a thing might be regarded as "opening up new frontiers" of the sport, but I imagine the real aim is a marketing demographic that emphatically does not include me. Either way, when you consider that this is supposed to represent a man fly fishing, it all seems a little trumped up and labored, like trying rather too hard to convince someone of the gritty physical perils and edgy rush of bowling.

The irreducible fact of fishing, of course, is water, and around water there hovers always the possibility of mishaps, sometimes serious ones. The big trout rivers of the West, slippery, swift, and powerful, do injure people and, more rarely, kill someone, though most often the river is only incidental to something else—strong drink or a weak heart. Remote as the danger may be, particularly if you refuse to court it, it is nonetheless real on rivers of any size. No such risks lurk on the small spring creeks of the Midwest, however; they pose no threat to life or limb. They inflict no harm but, like fly fishing itself, merely visit a thousand humiliations upon your head. All important things in life possess the capacity to humble you, and there is little wonder that a spring-creek fisherman quickly learns to address the water from his knees.

In seeing these special harmonies between fly fishing and spring creeks, I may be guilty of a type of self-deception that elevates personal quirks to the level of general principle. But I don't believe so, not entirely anyway, and the reason has to do with the way in which we come to our passions in life. You can be led in their general direction, but you arrive at them on your own. Some of the principles and ideas and skills, of course, are transmittable. In fishing, you can be shown how to cast, to set the hook, to maintain a tight line and play a trout—but these are only mechanics, and their mere implementation cannot be called fishing any more than vibrating air can be called music. The fishing exists elsewhere, in the cracks between these other things or somewhere underneath them: in the capacity to imagine in three dimensions, to infer the details of current and streambed from the character of the surface; in finding fish and reading their moods from the language of position, attitude, and movement; in sensing the take of a nymph or interpreting the drift or drag of a dry fly; in always having another idea; in a hundred other subtleties so automatic that you come to regard them as instinct, and only in retrospect realize that there was a time when you did not know them. And these cannot be passed along from a person who has them to one who does not; they fall into that large category of things in life that can be learned but cannot be taught.

Years ago there was a theoretical idea, "ontogeny recapitulates phylogeny," that briefly held sway in evolutionary biology. It posited that during embryonic development, the individual reenacts the history of the species, that we pass through the evolutionary forms that gave rise to us. Though now discredited as a principle of physiology, this notion describes, I think, a fundamental fact of human experience: we begin our lives by retracing the past. We find our way to those things that engage us most deeply in a process that is both discovery and rediscovery. Those in love, for instance, particularly in a first love, believe that they invented the whole affair, brought into being something never before felt by anyone on earth, and in a sense they are right. I still believe that I discovered every trout stream I ever fished, regardless of who or how many had been there before me. From the hodgepodge at hand, the raw materials of history and local circumstance, every devotee constructs his passion and in so doing makes it his own. You can see this as simply gaining knowledge and skill, but the feeling is less like acquiring something than creating it. Every fisherman reinvents the sport in just the way every child reinvents the language or every storyteller the story each time it is told. To fly fish a spring creek is to rediscover the modern origins of the sport, to recapture the logic of its form by reproducing the circumstances that first gave it shape. It is the reinvention of a method precisely calibrated to a place, the redrafting of an architecture, not merely through imitation but by rebuilding its very rationale.

If, of course, you have only the faintest blueprint and the crudest of materials with which to work, the finished structure is not always up to code. You may update and remodel from time to time, but you pretty much inhabit it for life.

~~~~~~~~~~

Despite my own metaphor, I'm always amused when some fly-fishing expert solemnly refers to one's tackle as "tools," in part because I have never regarded my fishing as something quite so serious as to require tools, but also because the first fly rod I ever owned might be called a "tool" in the way that a twig scavenged by a chimpanzee to fish termites from a hole might be called a "tool"—that is, something crude, inefficient, and slightly better than nothing. The rod in question was a six-and-a-half-foot, solid-fiberglass wrecking bar manufactured by the South Bend Company of South Bend, Indiana. We had much in common actually, that rod and I, both midwesterners, both aspiring to the same thing, and it had about as much right to call itself a fly rod as I did to call myself a fly fisherman. Thick-butted, colored a dirty butterscotch, with a grip that purported to be cork but I believe was a badly disguised corn cob, it had the winning aesthetics of orthopedic shoes. In what must have a been a moment of great hilarity in South Bend, perhaps as a gag at the office Christmas party, some prankster had printed on the rod shaft just above the grip FOR #6 LINE, in precisely the kind of squared-off, draftsman's hand you would use to print information that was actually relevant to something. For a time, I believed that this designation was plucked arbitrarily from the universe of whole numbers, but many years later it occurred to me that it might in fact have been the final stroke in a more sinister code: 6'6"6wt—the Rod of the Beast, the Anticast.

The only clue to its operation was a perfunctory and equally cryptic pamphlet written and illustrated in a terse Department of Agriculture style. As I remember, it contained a line drawing of an angler, rod poised at ten o'clock, captioned "The 'ready' position for the cast." This was immediately followed by another drawing, identical to the first, captioned, "The completion of the cast." The text was similarly instructive. But I would periodically haul this pamphlet, and the fiberglass rugbeater to which it allegedly bore reference, out into the backyard and exhaust myself with half an hour's worth of vigorous whippings, which I thought of as "practice." The first creature I landed on this tackle proved to be a small boy, inadvertently pinned between the shoulder blades on a backcast. Though in plump and prime condition, he did not fight well and instead curdled to the turf in a terrified, shrieking heap. Fearing that at any moment an enraged parent would appear and grind me to paste, I rushed to this shivering little mass and put my arm around it and begged it to stop. But it would not be reasoned with, or comforted, or, in the end, even bribed, and so I snatched the fly from the back of my victim, still prostrate with sobs and, exercising the better part of valor, fled the field.

The vision of this rod still haunts me, not because I will never forget it but because I cannot. That in the end I managed to catch a few trout with it is little short of miraculous. The first of these came on Emerald Creek. I was fishing what might be termed an accidental dry fly, a distantly recognizable version of a Black Gnat that I had tied myself, a classic wet fly that for some reason could not be made to sink. The trout struck in an unnecessarily violent slash-and-turn rise that left us mutually astonished. I had never seen such a thing happen before; the thrill was stunning and electric— like being struck in the zipper by lightning—and even now, the surface take of a trout still generates this same sensation, though in somewhat lower voltages. The strength of the fish surprised me, but I meant to have it, and did, a foot-long, amber-colored brown trout. I knocked it over the head and cleaned it, and when I laid open the flaps of its belly, the translucent orange flesh glowed like a slice of ripe cantaloupe—the indisputable mark of what we called a "native." I would learn later that such a trout, though streamborn and wild, was no more native to the place than I was.

The indigenous trout of the driftless area is the brook trout, and if its common name accords well with this place of countless little creeks, the scientific designation is more fitting still: *fontinalis*, "of the springs." The brook trout is often said to be the most beautiful of all trout species, and I will concede that it is colorful, almost improbably so, decked out in the kind of composite chromatics you might expect from a committee of hyperactive first graders turned loose on a box of crayons. It is, however, imaginatively done, and the only species of freshwater fish I know of that would not look out of place among the phantasmagoria of a coral reef. It possesses the most magnificent of tails, broad and square and elegantly proportioned, like the sail of a clipper ship. Brook trout still exist, though hardly thrive, in a handful of places in the driftless area—in the small, overgrown, unfishable upper reaches of some creeks, and even in the main stems of a few of the least known of these little-known waters. I do not fish for them deliberately but am delighted whenever I catch one, not because of their rarity but because they are a reminder that the past is not necessarily gone simply because it's behind you. The brook trout reflect the original circumstances of the place, and that is their beauty to me.

As in a great many waters of the eastern United States, the brook trout in driftless country were displaced by European invaders, the brown trout, the trout of Halford and Skues. Like the immigrants who introduced them, these transplanted trout flourished in their new surroundings by eradicating the native inhabitants and appropriating their territory. Brown trout are well suited to the spring creeks of the Midwest and particularly to the present condition of those streams. More robust than brook trout, they thrive in landscapes under the plow, in water that has been warmed by the engines of agriculture. They will subdue a population of brook trout, in part by eating it, though despite their aggressiveness in this respect, browns can be difficult to catch—a criticism lodged against their original introduction by anglers accustomed to the easy pickings of gullible native fish.

It is unfortunate, for a number of reasons, that the indiscriminate stocking of a nonnative fish was not halted by outrage
over their unsuitability as angling fare; at the least, it would
have furnished the cynical gratification of seeing one form of
stupidity being defeated by another, still deeper, form.

Depending upon your point of view, it is a sign of matu-
rity or arrogance or decadence that there comes a point in an
angling life when a fisherman abandons the quest for size and
numbers of trout and insists instead only on their difficulty.
The brown trout obliges. As fly fishing is the most demanding of methods, the brown trout is the most exacting of
trouts. Under certain circumstances, of course, even rainbow, brook, and cutthroat trout can grow fussy and will scru-
tinize a fly with the fastidious skepticism of an Amsterdam
diamond trader. But the brown trout is different. Many years
ago, I took a course in linguistics, memorable chiefly for the
fact that I understood none of it. But I do recall my teacher attempting to illustrate the great variations in the cultural psy-
chology by which names are given to things. He noted, as one
example, a small group of people that inhabited an atoll, in
Micronesia I think, who like those in many island societies
made a living from the sea. You would think, he suggested,
that such a culture would have developed a sophisticated taxonomy for things that lived in the ocean, relying upon them
as they did for food, tools, deities, and so on. But in fact the
language contained only two words for marine creatures—
one that designated things you could eat, the other things
that could eat you. The brown trout, I think, holds a similar
worldview and regards both categories with equal caution.
When a brown trout levitates from the streambed, slowly and
balloonlike, and drifts downstream eye to eye with your fly,
you get the distinct and uneasy impression that it's not just
looking, it's thinking.

Trout, of course, are not intelligent creatures, at least as the term is most often understood; they are merely but marvelously fitted to their world, though as in all populations, some individuals are less fit than others. And these were our first victims—the indiscreet, the witless, the chronically disaffected, the starving and the gluttonous, the impulsive, the slothful, the morally deficient and the mortally curious, the sediment at the bottom of the gene pool. For obvious reasons, fish of this sort grow neither large nor numerous, figuring far less prominently in the stream than they did in my creel. As each fly fisherman reinvents the sport, so the sport in turn invents each fisherman, its particulars shaping the outline of the angler he will one day be, piping the tune that first set the atoms of the brain to dancing. It was inevitable, then, that I would become, as I am, a fisherman of uncommonly low expectations, untroubled by size or numbers, not easily disappointed. In the modern age of high-octane angling, this is not a fashionable attitude—I don't find it especially praiseworthy myself—but it is a legacy of the past, willed to me by my own experience, and as matters stand with trout streams today, it sometimes comes in handy. This is not to imply that I don't care about catching fish; in the end, it may not matter much, but if you don't care about catching fish, you have no business fishing in the first place. I do have my vanities, but catching a lot of trout is not one of them.

Nor is catching the big one. I am not and have never been a big-fish fisherman, though it is not for want of effort. I had my day slavishly reproducing all the magazine-story antics. Operating under the big-trout-want-a-mouthful theory, I attempted to tease them to oversized streamers; then, under the big-trout-are-persnickety theory, I tried to coax them to tiny flies. I hunted for them and laid in wait at their lairs and once, this on a spring creek in Virginia, stalked a particular trout over the course of two seasons. It was an unusual fish of at least eighteen inches and probably closer to twenty, re-markable enough in this small stream, that had comman-deered an even more unlikely position—in the shallow tailout below a little one-lane bridge. The current had scoured a deep pool some twenty feet above the bridge and, its force expended, flowed leisurely past the wooden pilings and fanned out over a broad flat perhaps eight inches deep, the bottom a uniform sheet of coarse sand and tiny pebbles. There were no weeds or rocks or irregularities on the streambed, no overhead cover, no chute of current to funnel food, nothing at all about the spot that would seem appealing to a fish, but right there in the middle of all that nothing, ridiculously exposed to everything, was a single, quite re-spectable brown trout.

With elbows propped on the bridge railing, I watched that fish many times. Most of the trout we see are those brought to hand, and we become accustomed to looking at them in profile, admiring their shape and color. But this isn't really their best side. Trout are loveliest when viewed from above, where the brilliance of their design and the logic of camou-flage is most apparent. A fish in hand is like a jaguar or zebra in a zoo—out of context, its patterning is an absurdity—but against the background of its habitat, the coloration and markings are unexpected genius. A trout is almost supernat-urally sensitive to movement overhead, but if you sneak into the right position, you can watch a fish finning in the cur-rent, behaving like a thing unobserved. If you look long enough, you eventually see a speck drifting downcurrent, some unidentifiable anomaly—a bit of cottonwood fluff maybe, or a curled flake of leaf, or perhaps a mayfly—and you lean forward and squint, trying to make out if it is something alive. And when it gets close enough, the trout does exactly the same thing, straining slightly upward and forward to get a better view, its whole body language indicating that the fish is asking the same question. And you feel like you just might be on the right track after all.

The trout below the bridge, though, never appeared to be actively feeding. Now and again it would open its mouth in a white wink to nip something from the drift, but most of the time it didn't do much of anything, just swept its tail in a slow arc to hold in the current. It evidently had the one thing it wanted—a perfect view of the bridge, the one spot from which any approach to its location must commence.

When I finally decided to take a crack at that trout, I set about it in the predictable fashion, walked a short piece down the road, headed cross-country downstream, cut back to the creek, and crept up on the fish from behind. It had vanished. At least eight or ten times over the next two seasons, this basic scenario repeated itself. I tried at dawn and then at dusk a few times, hoping to give myself an edge with light, but the trout was never around; for whatever inconceivable reason, it appeared to take up a station below the bridge only during the hours of high sun. Sometimes I wouldn't see the fish on two or three consecutive trips and would conclude that someone had finally caught it. But then the next time out, it would be there again, or at least I presumed it was the same fish, since the choice of water was so idiosyncratic. Each time I stalked it, I walked a little farther down the road, cut a wider circuit around the fish, and struck the creek at a greater distance downstream, until at last I was traveling better than half a mile to end up less than one hundred feet from where I started. In all those attempts, I managed just two casts to that trout. Both times it spooked before my line ever touched the water.

Difficult fishing like this is supposed to teach you something, and indeed I learned that I was not any good at it. So I returned to fishing my accustomed water in my usual slapdash fashion, and my sole concession to catching large trout became the intermittent but sincere hope that I would luck into one. I realize that this is not very "technical," or "scientific," or "predatory," and no one knows better than I that it is not very "successful" either. In fact, the only surprising thing about it is that it sometimes works, albeit infrequently, but still more often than I deserve. I have hooked my share of large fish, and my share has been, in all justice, small.

In the driftless area, in fact, I was attached to a truly big trout only once, on a fishing weekend with an occasional companion named Duncan, who was a terrible fisherman but a good-natured and enthusiastic partner. He took great personal satisfaction in carrying around an aluminum-hooped trout net that he kept clipped to his belt, which always puzzled me, since most of the trout we caught could have been landed in a tea strainer. The fishing at Jerusalem Creek had been slow that morning, and we left early to scout out a place we had in mind; halfway there, we decided to make a quick detour to another stream, Amity Creek, that I'd found on the map. It did not look promising when we arrived, a tiny brook with banks choked in tall weeds, saplings, and brush. We walked a few hundred yards upstream along the edge of a cornfield, but the only water open enough to fish proved to be the pool beneath the bridge where we'd parked. We rigged for deep running, and on the second or third cast, I hooked into something I could tell was only huge and alive, a thing that moved with the same implacable sense of its own size as a city bus easing into traffic. Still new to trout fishing, I was unequipped in every respect for this turn of events. I gained a little line whenever the fish swam toward me, but at the end of several minutes, the best I could manage was a static tug of war. Like all neophytes with a big fish, I grew more fearful by the second of losing it, and when the standoff become unbearable, I applied as much pressure as I dared. The fish gave ground slowly, with a kind of resistance I'd never felt before, and when it came into sight at last, I saw why. Unwilling to have its head raised, it was boring straight for the bottom, and I was drawing it up tail-first, though the fish was, without a doubt, fair-hooked. When that tail finally broke the surface, it was bigger than a whisk broom, with a row of nickel-sized orange spots running down the flank and disappearing into the murky water. It gave a single, fierce slap and was gone.

I looked up at Duncan, who could only whisper a wide-eyed "Sweet Jesus."

I can still see that tail as clearly now as I did then. Since that time, I've caught a reasonable number of steelhead and grown somewhat accustomed to handling fish of decent size. Even adjusting for the windage and elevation of memory, I would confidently estimate that brown to have weighed better than eight pounds, living in a pool no bigger than a tollbooth. During the course of every angling life, the image of a few, particular fish are inscribed on the fleshy tablets of the brain. This was my first.

〰〰〰

Of all the spring creeks in the driftless area, none has more profoundly shaped my taste in trout streams than Emerald Creek. Each angler, I think, constructs from the stuff of his experience a Platonic trout stream that winds through the landscape of his imagination, the place against which all others are measured, the water he hopes to go to when he dies. Mine looks much like Emerald Creek. A nearly perfect miniature of my ideal, it is among the most visually serene places that I know, a consummate study in green. In its upper reaches, near the head of the valley, the stream hugs the foot of a limestone hill and runs almost invisibly in the deep shade of oak, sugar maple, and basswood. There is a large spring here, or perhaps an upwelling of groundwater through the streambed gravels, at the bottom of a deep run; if you wet-wade upstream, as we often did, you can feel the water grow cooler as you get near it. I once took two brook trout from this spot, identical twins all of ten inches and still the largest trout of their kind I've caught in spring-creek country. Farther down, the creek meanders through level meadows inlaid in places with angular, dark-green patches of planted corn, but most of it left to its own anarchic mix of grasses, wildflowers, and high weeds. Here, the course of the creek is clearly marked by a thin band of mature trees—more oak and maple, a scattering of walnut and locust—flanking the stream as though drawn down from the slopes by the fact of running water. The trees grow only along the banks, and the branches laced overhead form a low, vaulted canopy. The undergrowth is low and richly textured: the deckle of ferns; horsetails of both the feathery and phallic varieties; scalloped leaves of columbine; the weave of bindweed. Under a high summer sun, this surround of vegetation produces an extraordinary, viridescent light, a hundred shades of green, filtered and soft like light coming through stained glass. It stays cool in these green corridors, even on the hottest days, and stirs with just a breath of air on the windiest. At irregular intervals, the channel cuts an oxbow out beyond the streamside trees and into the meadow, carving a cutbank that edges a small and perfect bend pool. Meadow plants grow right up to the edge of the water, grasses mingled with clusters of goldenrod, tall stands of nettle, scatterings of milkweed, tangles of vetch, and a towering plant, coarse and woolly stalked, that is locally called cow parsnip, though cows won't eat it. If the stem is fractured, it bleeds a thick, virulent sap, and even a small amount on the skin will raise a blistery chemical burn that will not heal for months.

In its lowermost reaches, Emerald Creek winds through a few acres of open grassland colonized here and there by a single large oak, or a small grove of them, perhaps a remnant of oak savanna, though I may be only wishing it were so, that some fragment of the original landscape has managed to hold on here. I've spent a few fruitless nights prowling this section for a hatch of *Hexagenia* mayflies, but they've never once materialized. The stream is slower and deeper—the most difficult water on a spring creek to fish with flies. There are big trout here, but not many, and they are not the kind you simply fish for; they are the kind you mount a campaign against.

Emerald Creek itself is a green among greens, lush with aquatic plants. They grow in great variety and profusion almost everywhere, but nowhere do they swamp the channel in the manner of some English chalkstreams, where the sheer volume of weed displaces the water right over the banks. Here the vegetation is rich, but restrained. *Ranunculus*, the water crowfoot, flourishes in thick clumps; the leafy tendrils strain out waterborne sediments, which settle to the bottom in mounds of silt and sand at the base of the plants. Behind the mounds, the current scoops out hollows in the streambed, perfect places for trout but unfishable beneath a ceiling of wavering *Ranunculus* fronds that may trail ten or fifteen feet downstream of their roots. These leafy streamers, of a green so deep it is almost black, are sometimes drawn by the current into slow bend pools of viridian-tinted water, forming dark streaks and swirls like veins in a piece of polished malachite. Under a summer sun, such pools glow as though lit from within. Elodea takes hold in slower stretches, its brushlike whorl of translucent leaves a great favorite with snails. In slackwater coves, the stalks of arrowhead push above the surface and spread broad, chevroned leaves, like stylized birds in a painting. Fountain mosses cling to the rocks in riffly stretches, and at many places, dense mats of watercress grow outward from both banks and converge on the middle of the stream. The tangle of their succulent stems looks solid enough to walk on, though it is, I assure you, not. There are others—yellow-green patches of a plant that I suspect is water hypnum and the lobed, shell-like thallus of what must be some semiaquatic liverwort. But no good field guide to aquatic plants exists, at least none that I have found, and many species remain a mystery to me, including one of the most striking of all that finds a foothold only in the swifter, shallow flows—a flat, thumb-shaped leaf of a delicate bright green that borders on chartreuse, the color of spring lettuce. There is a particular bridge over the creek, lightly enough traveled so that you can stand on the roadway without being disturbed. Leaning on the railing, you look upstream at a stunning mosaic of aquatic vegetation, a collage of greens that run the spectrum from nearly blue to almost yellow, and every color kept bright by the constant wash of current. Weaving through this patchwork of plants are slender channels of shallow water over a pale gold bottom of limestone gravel and sand. It is one of the most restful prospects I have ever laid eyes on.

Emerald Creek, as I have said, is small, averaging maybe twelve feet in width, and from the fishing standpoint, this is pretty close quarters. It offers little in the way of backcasting room, only the low, open alleys over the water itself, and these are made almost uselessly short by the continual turning of the stream. To this day, I have never fished a place that required a more constant attention to one's vegetative surroundings. Because I learned how to fly fish under these circumstances, or learned at least well enough to catch a few trout, I never developed into much of a caster, having trained myself early to a certain cramped and fearful style. Much of the time, getting a fly on the water at all was an awkward, ad-libbed operation and occasionally required the kind of preposterous improvisation that one sometimes resorts to in using the rest room on a commercial aircraft. But in justice to myself I was not, in the matter of technique, an irredeemably bad caster; I was something perhaps worse and certainly more enduring—a choker. A defect of nerves, it is more difficult to remedy than a want of skill. I have tried, and even now, when the fishing is slow, I will visualize a trout rising in some difficult place—maybe in the small slick behind a hemlock stalk trailing next to the bank—then measure out the cast, and try to drop the fly precisely on the money in one shot. It is a foolish little game, like a kid shooting hoops in his driveway, counting down the seconds aloud, astounding the crowd with a stylish move, then launching the game-winning shot as time expires. You can reproduce everything but the one crucial element: pressure. Even so, I connect only about a third of the time in these little fictions, which is still a full third more than I manage in the real McCoy. And the size of the trout makes no difference; I will blow it equally with a six-incher or six-pounder.

But it is, I suppose, human nature to be drawn to the ruinous act. And mine is this, or one of a hundred like it: in the middle of Emerald Creek, there is an open spot where the water emerges from the trees; an overgrown two-track runs right up to it. The stream here is about ten feet across; watercress crowds in thickly from either bank, constricting the flow to a foot-wide channel that winds downstream through the vegetation for a distance of fifteen or twenty feet. At the head of this channel and a short way down into it, trout rise freely, often for much of the day. They appear to be small fish, though I've never been able to confirm this positively, and it is true that the rise of a large trout will at times resemble nothing so much as the rise of a small one. But the number of rings and their proximity to one another suggest little fish, highly selective feeders in a tight spot. Certain spring creeks produce these creatures, the worst of both worlds: small trout, but precociously discriminating, skeptical beyond their years, difficult to impress. They remind me of my nephew who, at the normally gullible age of four, was deeply unmoved by my legendary disappearing-dime trick. "It's still in your hand," he said, walking off.

These fish, in fact, must take the blame for my first foray into the arcana of trout-stream insects. If I could not improve my presentation, I thought, I might at least botch things with a better fly, and so began to study what the fish were eating. It proved a short course. The only bugs in the vicinity appeared to be dark and quite small, though it was difficult to tell at a distance. So I returned on one occasion with a little aquarium net. In what is a form of intelligence for some and exactly the opposite for me, I dipped the net just deep enough to pierce the surface film, held it there for a full minute, and then spread it out against my hand. It looked like the windshield of a pickup truck after an all-night drive, plastered with the crumpled hulls of a thousand insects, none more recognizable than a swatted mosquito. I rinsed a few into the white lid of a yogurt container, and the water ballooned out the delicate exoskeletons into the simulacra of living things. They were, as it turned out, dark and quite small, at which point I had taken the thing about as far as I could. My father once told me that you can give a cello to a monkey but that does not make him Pablo Casals, and this is the way stream entomology goes for me even now. It yields only the bracing confirmation that what appeared to be a mystery at first is indeed a mystery.

But I have always been helpless in the presence of rising trout. I am incapable of passing them by, even these small ones, even when they transform that first flush of hope into misgiving, then into impatience and frustration, and finally to a yellow-eyed, barking madness. Try to get within twenty feet of these little fish, and they spook; at twenty-five feet, the mere thought of a cast, flitting through your mind, puts them down; you begin to have a chance only beyond thirty-five feet. This is not a great distance, but you must cover it from your knees, and everything must be perfect—the cast, the drift, the fly—because there is only one opportunity. You must lay the fly line over the intervening ground, the leader over the watercress, and place the fly in a spot the size of a dollar bill. Even then, you might get twelve inches of drag-free drift before fly, leader, and line are impossibly tangled in weeds and watercress. Any attempt to free them invariably spooks the fish.

As a general principle, I have always found it valuable to distinguish between those things in life that offer a second chance and those that don't, but in this case the knowledge is crippling. It is a curious form of human perversity that, often enough, the studied precautions we take serve only to lead us to do the thing we fear most, in the way that desperate efforts to keep a lover can become the very jealousy that drives her off. Fishing these little fish, I begin to calculate too much, worrying about flushing them with a false cast, or lining them, or crashing the fly. This is the kind of fishing situation that is said to separate the men from the boys, and it never leaves me doubting which category I fit into. I have tried to raise these trout many times and would be better off trying to raise the dead. Still, I find it oddly consoling that in an age when "feeling good about yourself" has become a growth industry, fish care nothing for your self-esteem. It is one of their best qualities. Conversely, they have no particular stake in jerking you around either. Your errors are your own, the product of insufficient observation, inadequate physical skill, stupidity, or miscalculation. But these are finally small matters; for if individual trout snub you, a trout stream itself is nothing if not an endless series of second chances. Your successes too are your own, and they too are small, and wonderful for that since nothing palls faster than a string of jackpots.

Jerusalem Creek was the first spring creek I ever fished, but Emerald Creek remains my favorite. Even now, as I fish the big rivers of the West, I seek out the water that most closely resembles it—the gentle glide along a grassy bank; the light break of a riffle around the tip of an island, with that lovely, soft water on the inside; the braids and back channels—all those many small streams hidden within a large one, the secret places that feel to me like home.

These are the dances still danced by the atoms of my brain. All streams flow backward, and reflected somewhere in the surface of every river you fish are the images of those first places. "The present," writes Laurie Allman, "is just the past with some time on its hands." What is today but yesterday grown old? We are an architecture of our own recollection, and our lives are what hold it together. Even the body remembers. It is no coincidence that the salinity of blood and seawater are the same. When the first creatures first crawled out of Silurian oceans, primitive fish that we briefly resemble in gestation, they did not abandon the sea but wrapped a piece of it up in their skins and took it with them and passed it on to us. Like the earth, we are better than three-fourths water, with cells and tissues still nourished by tides that pulse seventy-two times a minute. The novelist Thomas Wolfe once wrote that "you can't go home again." The fact is, you can never leave. Whether an occasion for pleasant reverie or for a dose of Prozac and a twelve-step program, like it or not or both, we carry home in our heads.

5

The Land of Milk
and Honey

~~~~~~~~~~

The white kine glimmer'd, and the trees

Laid their dark arms about the field.

—Alfred Lord Tennyson, "In Memoriam"

I should confess now, though it
may be obvious already, that Jerusalem Creek and Emerald
Creek and the names I have used for all the streams are not
their real ones. Like all names, they are only convenient inventions, and in this case they serve not the communal convenience of a shared reference but the cravenly private one of
self-defense. I still fish these waters from time to time, and a
bulletproof vest doesn't hold many fly boxes. Even the most
genial anglers can get pretty testy if you start talking out
loud about their favorite waters, particularly when many of

those places are obscure and have so far escaped the calamities of a reputation. Granted, guidebooks to the region already exist, and one or two of them, written by local anglers with genuine credentials, are detailed and revealing. But even these people don't come clean entirely. Much is left unsaid, and I don't want to be the one to say it. So I consider this matter of names a necessary deception and infinitely preferable to life in the witness-protection program.

My precautions are probably unwarranted. In a great many respects, the spring creeks here offer little to draw fishermen from any distance and would not register at all on the radar of that curious creature that has proliferated in recent years, "the destination angler," whose aim in life is to cherry-pick the elite waters of the world. There is no fishing here at all on that scale, and so no angling epicenter has emerged, no West Yellowstone or Jackson Hole or Roscoe, New York, no place where the orthodontist from Phoenix can touch down for a weekend and transform a suitcase full of money into trout. There's no want of water, but most of the spring creeks are small and short. An exceptional stream may have ten or twelve fishable miles; most offer half that, or less. And while there are local concentrations of creeks, the vast number of them are distributed more or less uniformly over a land area the size of Vermont. No single river or group of waters so far outshines the others that it could attract a crowd of fishermen to any specific place. As Gertrude Stein once said of Oakland, "There is no there there." The destination angler will find no destination, and certainly none of the amenities that inevitably sprout up in the aftermath of discovery—the posh lodges, legions of itinerant guides that drift in for the summer, the trout-themed bars and faux-rustic restaurants, antique boutiques, and quaint galleries festooned with bad wildlife art. The spring creeks couldn't tolerate any real density of fishermen anyway, and the kind of lemminglike madness that afflicts many western rivers is inconceivable here. You need a lot of room on small streams like these, and to grant it is, by and large, the prevailing local protocol. And if for some strange reason the driftless area were vaulted to celebrity, anglers would find themselves, by dint of their own numbers, paying for a decidedly inferior fishing experience.

Besides, most anglers dismiss the idea of traveling any distance or taking much trouble to catch small trout. The vendors of modern fly fishing—books, magazines, tackle companies—traffic in images of the extraordinary and have created a generation of anglers who look at a ten-inch trout, or a day full of them, as a disappointment. Everyone wants the trophy, which goes a good way toward explaining the state of contemporary angling; the better waters have become overcrowded, and at least part of the problem is that everybody fishes the same big-fish places on the same big-fish rivers for the same big fish. It accounts as well, I think, for a certain unpleasant and at times psychotic competitiveness that one is sometimes doomed to witness; there are only so many large trout to go around, and if you don't get yours, someone else will. The spring creeks of driftless country are not really big-fish waters, though they do hold some large trout, even very large ones. From time to time, in a small-town grocery store or tavern, you'll find a snapshot taped to the cash register, a blurry Polaroid of someone dangling a brown trout of seven or eight pounds from a stringer. But such fish are taken at night, on bait, and very, very infrequently. Most of the trout here are like most of the trout almost everywhere—small. A twelve-incher is a decent fish, fourteen a nice one, and you might expect the occasional sixteen-incher. Bigger ones are a possibility, but you could fish, say, the Bighorn River and catch more eighteen-inch trout in a week than you probably would in a lifetime on these spring creeks.

Some places, like the open meadows with low stream banks, are a joy to fish—easy walking and ample casting room—but most often, you earn whatever you get. The trout themselves are not abnormally difficult; they are like trout in many spring creeks—cooperative at times, but usually not. Rather, the fishing conditions can get surprisingly trying for a landscape that appears so pastoral and benign. As I have said, heavy vegetation and tight quarters put a premium on accurate and sometimes acrobatic casting, and the price of failure is lost flies or spooked trout. Tall banks and high weeds often force you into the stream to find backcasting room, and the wading can be laborious for such modest water. You hit stretches of bottom humped with marly knobs, slick as lard, and in places must push upstream through soupy thickets of aquatic weed. The going is slow, even strenuous at points, and managing it without flushing the fish requires determination and patience. Worst of all by far are the expanses of fine, mushy silt that blanket the bottom from bank to bank and extend downward, as far as I can tell, all the way to the center of the earth. I waded up onto just such a silty flat one day at the lower end of a long, gentle bend on Hummingbird Branch, one of those ideal places where the gradient of current speeds is so arranged that any decent cast will produce fifteen or twenty feet of drag-free drift. Just because it fished so well, I worked the water rather too long, and the slight shift of weight produced by the motions of casting wedged my right foot farther and farther into the mud until I was nearly knee-deep. Realizing at last that a situation just might be developing, I took a step forward, and the soft bottom swallowed my leg right up to the nethers, a descent that might well have continued indefinitely had not the toe of my boot, straining downward like a ballet dancer at full extension, finally come to rest on something solid—a broken chunk of limestone no doubt, but at the time I wondered if it might be the skull of another fisherman. All the usual tugging and pulling proved fruitless, and I finally freed myself by lobbing my rod up on the bank, flopping chest-down in the mud, and clawing my way out—an event not worth mentioning, I should point out, had it happened only once.

There are other deterrents. In the heat of high summer, the valleys fill with air so muggy that drawing breath is like inhaling wet velvet, and just stringing up a rod in the morning leaves you dripping in sweat; by early afternoon, your brain is making its own gravy. Seek shade and you find mosquitoes, an annoyance on even the hottest days, though nothing compared to the evenings, when they take a serious notion, indifferent to bug spray and bent on the tenderest spots—behind the ears, the corners of the eyes, the skin between the fingers. They can drive even my imperturbable brother to desperate measures. He used to carry with him a packet of indescribably cheap cigars or, more accurately, cigar-shaped objects composed of an anonymous shredded vegetable matter hydraulically shoved in a paper tube that was dyed and embossed to resemble tobacco leaf. When the mosquitoes became unbearable, he would torch up one of these abominations. To hold one in your mouth was to risk tasting it, which, judging by the odor, would be like licking the bottom of a bird cage. Instead, he contrived with great ingenuity to fasten this garbage fire to his hatband or creel strap when he fished, and I could always locate him by the plume of evil-colored smoke that wafted above the stream-side grasses. How many innocent creatures were exterminated on his downwind side is impossible to estimate.

There are red-winged blackbirds here, too, not ordinarily considered a menace, but with their preference for nesting in swampy areas and along watercourses, they converge on the spring creeks with an aggressive and ill-tempered territoriality, a short fuse, and Hitchcockian designs. Step too close, and no matter how innocently or quietly you transgress the invisible blackbird boundary, you call down upon your head a flurry of strafing wings, angry beaks, and clamorous cries that sound like someone assaulting a set of bagpipes with an axe handle. The problem is that these birds are tireless; they show none of a wild creature's usual skittishness and will not be frightened off or driven away. Fishing on Emerald Creek once, intent upon the water, I heard a rustling in the brush across and downstream, some distance away. I held very still, thinking at first it was a deer browsing up the bank. But it grew louder and more frantic as it approached, limbs shaking and branches snapping, when all at once my fishing partner burst from the bushes at a dead run, one hand clamped over his hat, pursued by a pair of these shrieking harpies bent on pecking him senseless. I've been hectored mercilessly by these birds on countless occasions, and it's not the threat but the insufferable relentlessness of it. Finally, like a caribou driven mad by a swarm of biting flies, you can't bear it anymore, and no matter how promising the water or good the fishing, you are forced to retreat, which I suppose for the birds is exactly the master plan.

Every fishing spot, of course, has disincentives, and I suppose on the larger scale, the oppressive air and the mud and the mosquitoes and the birds are minor irritations, not even registering in the top ten discomforts. In and of themselves they are insufficient to deter the destination angler, who is accustomed not only to more taxing obstacles—the fierce and icy winds of Tierra del Fuego, Labrador's vampirish black flies—but potentially lethal ones: Alaskan grizzly bears, Sikorsky helicopters, Scottish haggis. But he expects in return to be whisked off to the best spots on the best waters, to get instant fishing of the highest caliber. In the driftless area, he will find neither. It does not hold out the unspoiled fishing of truly wild places or the catered, upscale comforts of the civilized retreats that have sprung up all over the world. It is a kind of middle territory, of little consequence to modern angling's penchant for extremes. So I suppose I might have named the names of creeks and pinpointed my favorite waters in the reasonable certainty that few fishermen would travel very far to find them, that the streams would remain safe from the kind of infestation that has visited disaster on so many other trout rivers. You may read all the guide books in print, but finally these waters must be scouted out and discovered, each little stream looked into, explored, and learned, and the reward, in inches or avoirdupois, is modest. Figuring them out takes time, and time, practically by definition, is what a destination angler has least of. Spring-creek country is pretty much a do-it-yourself affair.

With that said, it is still undeniable that more people are doing it these days, and the streams, though far from crowded, are more heavily fished than they used to be. In the past, the hordes descended on opening day, as they do everywhere, to pillage a handful of streams stocked with trout. But they vanished in a week or two, as they do everywhere, and thereafter we rarely saw anyone fishing, let alone anyone using flies. I don't recall even seeing another fly angler until I was twenty-five and had already been fishing the driftless area for a decade. They were around, of course, but there weren't many. The number of fishermen here began to grow about the same time it began to grow everywhere else, boosted by an economic upturn, by the movie, and by whatever strange fuel it is that stokes the American fad machine. I understand that a few guides have even begun working the area in recent years, though only a few, and I have no idea whether they are making a go of it. But even now, you can almost always hunt up some unoccupied water and frequently find a whole creek to yourself; it just takes more effort than it once did. Most of the new anglers appear to be local, with a scattering from as far away as Minneapolis, Milwaukee, and Chicago, though I believe this last group in particular has been rather coolly received; the antipathy borne by rurals for the metropolitan invader crosses all boundaries. But the local fishermen I've met over the years are altogether likable people and classic midwesterners.

≈≈≈≈≈≈≈≈

The Midwest, as both a geographical and cultural entity, seems to be a source of confusion to many of my countrymen, who conceive of the region alphabetically rather than cartographically. There are a bunch of "I" states (Idaho sometimes gets thrown in the mix), and some "M" states (which may or may not include Montana, depending upon whom you talk to), and one of those "W" states, Wyoming perhaps. As a physical place, it is envisioned as a default zone, an area that doesn't border an ocean, has no deserts, and isn't the Rocky Mountains. I generally watch TV news with only one eye, which is half an eye more than it merits, but I'm sometimes startled to attention by the announcement of "violent storms pounding the Midwest" only to find out that tornadoes have touched down in Nebraska or Kansas or one of the Dakotas, which as every midwesterner knows are the Plains States. There is some dispute even among midwesterners whether Missouri and Ohio rightly belong to the region, the former often regarded as part of the South and the latter of the East, and the question is by no means settled. But there is no disagreement about the core of the place, a tier of three states on the south—Iowa, Illinois, Indiana—and a tier of three more bordering them on the north—Minnesota, Wisconsin, and Michigan. Still farther north is Canada, which is in some ways one giant midwestern state. Wisconsin, completely surrounded by the rest of the Midwest, can fairly lay claim to being the heartland of a region that is already the heartland of the nation, and though the state may not be precisely in the middle of the country, the human heart too is somewhat north and east of center.

These geographical misconceptions are of no great consequence except as a symptom and symbol of a more general sense of anonymity about the area. For it is precisely its "middleness" that renders the Midwest so generic to the rest of the country. It possesses no identifying extremes. It lacks the mystique of wilderness, the anachronistic charm of rural New England or colonial Virginia, and the big city's ceaseless onslaught of sensory input that is donned like armor against the greatest of all terrors in a leisure society—boredom. What remains is the perception that the Midwest is dismissible small potatoes, a place where nothing of real importance occurs, that it can be left to itself without much fear that it will one day demand attending to. In the large and dysfunctional national family, the Midwest is America's unexceptional child, well intentioned but bland, the one that collects bottle caps and bicycles a paper route, that dutifully practices the clarinet but never gets any better. This picture doesn't much bother midwesterners—by whom I mean primarily small-town people; beyond a certain size, cities become detached from a region and more nearly resemble one another than they do the surrounding territory. The people I grew up with and the ones in the Midwest that I still know regard their national image both with amusement, because they know it doesn't really fit, and with a certain secret pride, because they know it does. But for the most part they don't care about what other people think. Unpretentiousness is practically a regional fetish, and midwesterners look upon the self-important vanity and pathological narcissism of places like Los Angeles and Washington, D.C., in moral bewilderment and with great relief at their distance in both miles and manners. They are thankful not to live amid such provincialism.

Like most peoples, they are best known through their social establishments, and foremost among these are the taverns—a term used almost universally instead of "bar." A bar is merely a place to drink; a tavern participates more closely in communal life, and in some respects its closest analogue, though by no means a perfect one, is the rural English pub. Families go out to dinner at the taverns; small children and dogs weave among the table legs; men shake leather dice cups and upend them on the bar with a sharp slap; others play cribbage. The whole place is wrapped in an atmosphere of locality, with stuffed deer heads on the wall, illuminated beer signs, bowling trophies, mounted muskies, photos of the softball team, and miscellaneous tchotchkes, often of a North Woodsy sort. Any similarity to an English pub, however, ends with the beer, which is unspeakably lame and lifeless, the stuff excreted from industrial vats by the tankerload—the brewing equivalent of grocery-store white bread, which is, not coincidentally, another midwestern staple.

Old-timers order this beer in a quart bottle—termed a "tiny"—and for some unknown reason dispatch it by repeatedly filling and draining an eight-ounce juice glass, a practice that does not appear to have caught on among the younger patrons. Gallon jars of embalmed animal products sit on the bar within reach—pickled pigs' feet and ham hocks, pickled eggs, pickled kielbasa, all swimming in a cloudy brine—though I can't recall ever seeing a jar of just plain pickles. Their purpose extends beyond the obvious decorative value;

people actually eat these things. Somewhere on one of the walls hangs a deer cinch (sometimes called a bull cinch), a length of iron rod welded into the shape of the male symbol, like this ♂. It is a midwestern version of the jackalope, its sole function to have a chuckle at the expense of the credulous. Anyone inquiring into its purpose is treated to a lengthy explanation (abbreviated here), during which co-conspirators gather round, shoulders shaking in scarcely containable mirth. The substance of the story, usually told in tones that move deliberately from the offhand to the excited, is that you carry a deer cinch into the woods, sneak up behind a deer, and plant the arrow where the moon don't shine. If you can hang on to the ring, it's a cinch you got him. Pretty good, eh? Well, what do you know. It brings the house down every time, and besides, if you don't like it, there's other stuff—a couple of quarters epoxied to the bar, a little plastic donkey that dispenses toothpicks from its rear end, that kind of thing. It's a sense of humor more jokey than funny, but after a few beers, you start to get it.

The small-town Wisconsin taverns—the ones to which I have devoted most of my research—serve as informal headquarters for three quasi-sacred local institutions. The first is deer hunting, for which the passion is insatiable; in some places, mostly in the north, school is canceled on opening day. Second is the Friday-night fish fry, and taverns that take it seriously dish up only one variety—walleye—which I find the finest eating of all freshwater fishes, trout notwithstanding, and the only one cooked to best advantage when properly deep-fried. In the towns bordering Lake Michigan, the fish fry is sometimes supplemented with, and sometimes replaced by, the "fish boil," an enormous simmer of lake trout, potatoes, and onions that is better than it sounds, though not by much. Third is the Green Bay Packers, whose followers constitute the single largest religious denomination in the state;

Sunday is set aside for worship. A regional penchant for country music notwithstanding, polka is king here, and on a Saturday night, every Legion Hall and VFW in the state thumps to the sound of Jimmy Sturr on the jukebox or some local talent in a bolo tie and flowered shirt crushing "The Beer Barrel Polka" from a pearl-inlaid accordion the size of a Duesenberg engine.

Generalizations about regional characteristics, of course, are always problematic, and never more so than now, when geographical particularities are being hosed away by a high-pressure stream of homogenized images sprayed round the clock from TV cables and data ports. Still, I think that landscape does count, if only in smaller ways now, toward the formation of character, and that history and memory will put up resistance even in a losing battle. Some things endure, though if pressed, I am prepared to admit that this conviction may owe as much to my own parochial affections as to impartial study. In any case, midwesterners have always struck me as generous folks, quick to lend a hand even to strangers for the simple reason that it lies within their power to do so; I have never met people who adhere more strongly to an abstract sense of duty. While frequently regarded, and portrayed, as naïve, they are politically and culturally more sophisticated than they are often given credit for. An agricultural economy hinges on things much larger than a cornfield—world commodity prices, the politics of petroleum, fiscal practices of foreign governments, and a host of other variables that fluctuate with the winds not only of domestic administration but of global markets. And I rather suspect that there are many average small-town midwesterners who see more museums, attend more concerts, and visit more galleries in a year than many average New Yorkers. "Rural" is the equivalent of "uncultured" precisely as often as "urban" is equivalent to "cultured."

Still, there is no denying, or reason to deny, that the rural Midwest is predominantly a farm society with predominantly country attitudes and a straightforward, workmanlike view of life. What you see with them is pretty much what you get; the world is hard enough, they say, so why complicate it with elaborate systems of camouflage? This directness sometimes makes midwesterners seem moralistic and preceptive, and it is often enough true. They are compulsively friendly, and nothing if not polite, but candid too; if they believe you deserve it, they will make you feel their disapproval—politely, of course, and most often voiced in a words-to-the-wise tone. It may be the long and bitter winters that breed a kind of stoicism or endurance, though it is good-natured rather than dour, and it infuses the whole region with an oddly upbeat brand of Nordic Lutheranism. People tend to accept with equanimity, or at least resignation, the countless ways life has of underscoring human frailty—the inadvertent pregnancy, the lunatic uncle, the failed business. There is as well a brand of tolerance that goes beyond mere stoicism and is particularly surprising for rural people. One can find in even the smallest towns, for instance, the tattoos, nose rings, tongue studs, and other perforations of the nouveau gothic, and while these hardly pass without comment, neither are they an occasion for antagonism or ostracism, only a perfectly ordinary incredulity. The underlying assumption is that people are more alike than different, and the differences should not be allowed to obscure that fact—provided, of course, they are not too different.

Like rural people everywhere, midwesterners have an inexplicable affinity for straddling endless variants of the internal-combustion engine, which include but are not limited to dirt bikes, ATVs, Jet Skis (the most recent pestilence), and, particularly in Wisconsin, snowmobiles, which careen about at lethal speeds making slightly more noise than is humanly bearable. To be fair, I've never assumed the snowmobiler's principle motive to be the pure aggravation of his fellow man; that is merely the principle result. The brutal windchill encountered on these joy rides is held at bay by a predilection for brandy in almost any form: abergut (half brandy, half peppermint schnapps, also favored by cross-country skiers), peach brandy, apricot brandy, pear brandy, applejack, slivovitz, extra sharp ginger flavored brandy (ordered in a tavern acronymously as ESGFB), and even regular old brandy, but particularly Christian Brothers (locally known, with some affection, as "Brother Tim"). Every couple of winters, some brandied-up snowmobiler sieves his carcass through a barbed-wire fence at sixty miles per hour, and though I don't ordinarily take pleasure in the misfortune of my fellow man, I do respect justice in all its forms and wish that a similar court existed for the Jet Ski crowd.

In a state where every car advertises "America's Dairyland" on its license plate, eating cheese is a matter of civic responsibility. Next to sausage, it is considered nature's most perfect food and is consumed in unimaginable quantities—by itself or in a sandwich or melted over almost anything, including more cheese. Many of the cheeses are produced for the mass market, insipid varieties such as American, brick, and Colby, which, as far as I can tell, are specifically manufactured for people who don't like the taste of cheese. There are a few indifferent hard cheeses made here, Parmesan and Romano; some passable veined ones, particularly the Amish-made bleus and Gorgonzolas; and a few creditable Swisses. Recently, a number of artisanal farmstead makers have set up shops that craft boutique cheeses, mostly sheep- and goat-milk types, which I am told are quite good. But the undisputed sovereign of cheeses here is cheddar. The vast majority of it is bland and characterless, marketed to the commercial taste, but in some of the smaller cheeseries you can still find the premium stuff, transcendent cheddar that retains just a hint of the barnyard, aged for years to a crumbly, salty bite that will pucker your eyelids and produce the most pleasant ringing in your ears.

Despite the claims of state boosters, the first settlers did not arrive in the area, plant a flag on the highest hill, and announce, "We shall make cheese." As in many border areas, the first commercial farming efforts here were devoted to grain production. But when the wheat market collapsed in the panic of 1873, dairy-wise immigrants, some from Europe, most from New York State, stepped in to lead an agricultural retooling. By the turn of the century, the driftless area alone had hundreds of creameries and cheese factories, most sited at a crossroads where local farmers could conveniently deliver fresh milk each day. The factories were a natural for the area; remote valleys and hilly terrain made whole milk a slow, heavy, and perishable cargo, more easily preserved and transported as cheese, just as farmers in other parts of the country discovered that corn was simpler and more lucrative to ship if it was turned into whiskey first. Many of these small factories still exist, and you can stop in and buy, among other things, bags of curd, soft nugget-shaped pieces of a proto-cheese substance. A cheese curd emits a peculiar squeaking sound when you chew it—like biting a Styrofoam packing peanut—and doesn't taste like much of anything, least of all cheese. But they have a junk-food-style addictiveness, and I've driven endless miles scouting trout streams, making myself sick on curd.

There are fewer cheese factories now because there are fewer dairy farms, but the livelihoods of many people in driftless country are tied directly or indirectly to the ones that remain. Agriculture, by its very nature, leaves a large footprint on a place, and the cows and farms here remain such a fundamental presence that they have become for me one of the emblems of driftless country.

As to the cows themselves, I am strikingly ignorant for
one who spent half a lifetime in dairy country. In the third
grade we were obliged, as a matter of state pride, to learn the
names of the most important dairy cows—Holstein, Brown
Swiss, Guernsey, Jersey, and a few others I've forgotten—
though I understand now that the favored variety is a Hol-
stein-Friesian, from which a strong hand might squeeze fifty
pounds of milk a day. Regardless of breed, however, cows
have always appeared to me little more than ambulatory di-
gestive tracts, wrapped in cowhide and sprinkled with flies,
through which food endlessly passes. And in my experience,
one simply can't do better than "bovine" to characterize that
which is plodding, dull-witted, and terminally nonplussed.
To a dairy farmer, cows are the occasion of unremitting labor,
a crop that demands constant tending. They must, for instance, be milked on a regular schedule, usually twice a day,
or else . . . actually, I have no idea what would happen, but
horrible images spring to mind.

From the fishing standpoint, it would be better if cows
did not exist. They are notorious for cropping the edible
riparian vegetation, trampling the rest, and mashing the
earthen banks to a muddy pudding. Silt washes into the
stream and settles over everything, filling in the deep spots,
blanketing the spawning gravel, and suffocating aquatic
plants; the water warms; the trout languish. To blame the
cows for this, I suppose, is like faulting an ill-behaved dog for
the failings of its owner; they are only doing what cows do.
Some dairy farmers, to be fair, are mindful of the problem
and take precautions, and many spring creeks bear the scars
of repair and rehabilitation—bankside stabilization, artificial
in-stream structures, and other prosthetics that have restored
some measure of normal functioning. Others have not been
this lucky, lost through chronic neglect and, barring any
miraculous transformation in agricultural methods, probably
beyond reclamation. But the cows are a fact of the place, one

of the compromises of human occupation. If you can come to accept them, they do give the countryside a bucolic picturesqueness—perhaps not enough to offset the damage they do, but more compensation than you usually get from the agents of environmental degradation.

Cows, as animals, finally don't interest me much. But as the endpoint of a support network that extends outward to encompass not only the dairymen but farm-implement dealers, feed and seed salesmen, livestock brokers, bankers, and so on to the merchants that feed, house, and clothe everyone down the line, dairy cows and farms have been a dominant force in shaping both the cultural and the natural landscapes. They are evident in patterns of land usage and the particular version of nature that those patterns allow; in economics; in the structure of community; even in the rural architecture. Perhaps the most readily visible mark that cows have left on driftless country are the farmsteads themselves, and particularly the classic midwestern barn (it is in fact called the "Wisconsin barn") that is the unmistakable signature of a dairy farm. The building is one hundred feet long and a third as wide, often finished with either a double-pitched gambrel roof or an arched Gothic one to increase the volume of hay storage. The oldest ones have thick fieldstone foundations and are set with long rows of windows to admit light for feeding and milking. They are handsome structures, admirably fitted to their purpose, and they are not at all out of place in the landscape. Adjacent to the barns are silos, the older ones built of tile block or concrete, but more often these days a modern blue Harvestore. There are milk houses and sheds and, a short distance away, the farmhouse proper, sometimes of that large and rambling style with wraparound porches, built in prosperous times. The surrounding land is apportioned according to purpose—cornfields, woodlot, hayfields, pasture—although pastures are used less now as the smaller operations have gradually disappeared into consolidation. There are fewer farms working larger acreages, and a greater control exercised over what and where the stock is fed.

But the old pattern of smaller farms persists in miles of fencing that crisscross the valleys, much of it unnecessary now but easier to leave up than tear down. And in many places, fishing the spring creeks depends upon the dexterity with which you can climb over, wriggle under, or slip through barbed wire and the ease of conscience you can summon on the private property beyond. Like the fences, the roads here owe their character in part to the cows. Unlike many other rural regions, the driftless area has almost no gravel roads. Even the least-traveled country lanes, down the smallest valleys and up the winding coulees, are hard-surfaced because milk is picked up every few days by tank trucks that must make the rounds in the harshest and snowiest weather. But asphalt is about the only modern concession; many of the county blacktops, narrow, with no painted lines or gravel shoulders, follow the old wagon routes. Meadow grasses and wildflowers grow chest-high right up to the edge of the pavement, and driving down one of these back roads in midsummer gives the most pleasing sense of being recessed into the countryside.

The presence of people has changed the landscape but not obliterated it; spring-creek country remains a place inside the edge of nature. For all the alterations that have been worked on the land, there is an unexpected continuity as well, a driftless character even to many of these changes. Agriculture here has preserved, if only inadvertently, a rough kind of consistency, and the landscape still retains some of its original mid-Holocene character. The plateaus, the rolling hilltops, all the larger and flatter spaces once dominated by prairie still give the impression of grasslands in the fields of corn, wheat, and oats. On steeper ridges, the composition of the trees has changed, but the slopes are still wooded as they have been for millennia. The gentler hillsides and bottom-lands were once covered in oak savanna—groves of bur and white oak scattered in a mix of forbs and grasses, open, park-like places maintained by patterns of drought and wildfire. The true savannas have all but disappeared in the wake of fire suppression, but some semblance of them remains in places where oaks still stand and grazing cows perform the function of wildfire in keeping the understory clear. Perhaps these resemblances to a landscape of the past are only super-ficial, but I do not see it as coincidence that human patterns of use should sometimes mirror natural ones, and it would doubtless be a better thing if it happened more often.

These artifacts of human occupation, set in their particu-lar natural surroundings, give this land its distinctive feel—it is a place on the border, a domesticated landscape, a middle ground between nature and culture. And a small herd of Hol-steins, scattered about a pasture, is both the agent of that ne-gotiation and one of the emblems of the space it has created.

On one of the streams we used to fish often, there was a stretch of pasture along one bank, upstream from a small bridge. The channel ran close to the foot of a ridge, leaving just enough room between them for a rutted dirt two-track that ran in fifty or sixty yards from the valley road. At the end of the two-track, ten feet from the bank opposite the pas-ture, someone had set up five beehives. They had apparently been there for years; a couple of them were no longer quite level, the ground beneath them having heaved and settled over time, and the others were shimmed to plumb by slats of barn siding and scraps of two-by-four. They were ordinary white bee boxes, maintained but not fussed over, the province of an experienced beekeeper. As you watched the hives over the course of a summer, they gradually rose taller as the keeper (whom we never saw) added supers, the shallow topmost frames where honey is stored, to meet the growing need for space as an annual succession of flowering plants and trees came into season.

I always looked forward to fishing this stretch; with the bees on one side, the cows on the other, and the creek up the middle, it made a most charming pastoral scene. I particularly liked the hives, for keeping bees was once a great desire of mine, and by the age of nine or so I'd undertaken what I considered a serious course of self-study on the subject. Even then I recognized that most people were made uneasy by the idea of thirty or forty thousand bees in close proximity, and that obtaining a hive would require more than just the usual begging and whining. So, I took a long and objective look at my parents, weighed the prospects, and then launched my first tactically sophisticated, psychologically deliberate, prolonged adult-style siege—pressing my case at the crucial moments; lying low at others; giving a little behind-the-scenes push here, a gentle unobserved steering there; always alert and sensitive to how the notion was percolating with my father, for he was already an avid gardener and the linchpin of my plan. Secure his cooperation and any local resistance would fall. A model of patience and strategy executed over the better part of a year, my scheme was just beginning to bear fruit when my father moved the family to a larger city, where beekeeping would be logistically and, I suspect, legally impossible. I've been beeless ever since, but have maintained an interest in them over the years, continued to read about them, though in a sporadic and amateur fashion, and for most of my adult life have numbered a beekeeper or two among my casual acquaintances. Driftless country is not known as a honey-producing area, nor is hobbyist beekeeping more popular here than elsewhere, but because these five hives were the first I ever saw close up, honeybees became woven deeply into the feeling of the place.

A bee box is a cunning structure; it doesn't attempt to force the bees to do anything, but rather channels their instincts and natural proclivities to a beekeeper-friendly format—allowing him to perform routine maintenance and honey removal without destroying the hive or even upsetting the bees much. The movable-frame hive was the invention of one Reverend Lorenzo Langstroth, a nineteenth-century American apiarist. He was an eccentric and complicated character—possibly, some have suggested, subject to bouts of manic-depressive illness—and his remarkable insights into bees show that kind of uncanny genius, essentially artistic in nature, that sometimes allies itself with the off-center personality. Such people do not often lead happy lives, and Langstroth's seemed troubled at many points. He was a bit of a crank, unable to conceal his exasperation with anyone who did not observe and appreciate scientific method, and merciless toward fools, charlatans, and the peddlers of "patent hives." But his book *The Hive and the Honeybee* is a masterpiece of exact and exacting observation and a thoroughly engrossing read.

Langstroth, for instance, was the first to articulate in practical detail the notion of "bee space," one of the concepts around which he designed his revolutionary form of hive. In a hive, bees confronted with a space wider than three-eighths of an inch will attempt to build comb in it; faced with a space of less than a quarter inch in width, the bees will seal it with propolis, a kind of glue made from plant resin. Langstroth built his hive with an intermediate gap, about five-sixteenths of an inch, between the frames and hive body and arranged the interior frames so that, when filled with comb, this same space would remain between them. This bee space is too small to prompt the building of comb and too large to glue together; it maximizes the amount of honey stored in the hive and simplifies its removal for the keeper. It gives the bees a kind of optimal personal space and the colony a communal comfort zone, and I have often wondered if there is some human analogue.

Langstroth is at his most captivating, though, when he writes about the personality and the mood of his bees, which he interprets from the sound of the hive and the behavior of its occupants. His remarks are fascinating from a naturalist's point of view, but what stands out most vividly in his accounts is the depth and complexity he ascribes to his bees, and the sympathy he feels for their inner lives. Listen to him on bees discovering the loss of their queen:

> At such times, instead of calmly conversing, by touching each other's antennae, they may be seen violently striking them together, and by the most impassioned demonstrations manifesting their agony and despair.

Or this, on robber bees that steal honey from another hive:

> There is . . . an air of roguery about a thieving bee which, to the expert, is as characteristic as are the motions of a pickpocket to a skillful policeman. Its sneaking look, and nervous, guilty agitation, once seen, can never be mistaken.

Or this, on his experiment in which a new, empty hive was introduced in place of the old one while the workers were out gathering nectar:

> Thousands of workers which were ranging the fields, or which left the old hive after its removal, returned to the

familiar spot. It was truly affecting to witness their grief and despair; they flew in restless circles about the place where once stood their happy home, entering the empty hive continually, and expressing, in various ways, their lamentations over such a cruel bereavement.

This is, albeit in a slightly batty way, magnificent stuff. The passionate fanaticism, the affection, the unapologetic anthropomorphizing, all remind me of nothing so much as the way fishermen speak about fish.

It isn't difficult to see why Langstroth was so taken, for bees are fascinating creatures. As spring creeks are rare among rivers, so honeybees are rare among bee species, for they are a social insect that lives in colonies. While often described as a society in which the queen bee rules over the workers, a colony is not really a monarchy; there are no courtiers or cardinals, barons or bishops, or any of the other descending echelons of ass kissers that attend the true hierarchical order; there is only the queen, more a prisoner than royal personage, though I suppose historically a great many sovereigns have been both. But a hive finally looks to me less like a society than a form of cult. Much has been made of the industry and busyness of bees and the tireless, coordinated activity of the colony, which in the larger scheme is an accurate description. On a smaller scale, however, people who study individual bees have found that a field worker spends, on average, less than four hours a day on the job—and that's not even continuous, but broken up by periods of loafing and napping. Precisely this same figure, four hours, corresponds to an estimate I once read of how much time a day was spent by "primitive" hunter-gatherers in acquiring the necessities of life. I find this correspondence most suggestive and its implications highly appealing. It offers some indication of which direction to head in pursuit of the zero-hour workweek.

As nearly everyone knows, a most unusual characteristic of honeybees is their capacity for complex communication. When a worker locates a source of nectar, she returns to the hive and performs a sort of dance, moving about in a set of choreographed steps while wiggling her abdomen and touching antennae with a crowd of surrounding bees. She conveys in this way the type and amount of nectar, its range and bearing from the hive, and as a result the appropriate number of workers are dispatched to the right location. Virtually every animal, of course, can communicate to some degree with one of its own kind, if only for the rudimentary purposes of procreation, but distance, direction, and quantity—these are sophisticated concepts. Honeybees, I am given to understand, are unique among insects in this way, sharing a language capable of expressing abstract ideas, though apparently all they talk about is food.

Of all the features of a hive, the comb is perhaps the most aesthetically appealing. A regular arrangement of identical hexagons, it is an elegant structure, in part because the hexagon itself is a shape of intrinsic balance and repose, and one that crops up in unexpected and sometimes archetypal contexts: six atoms of carbon, the organic element from which all life stems, join to form the hexagonal benzene ring; the 120-degree interior angle of a hexagon is prevalent in cellular structures throughout nature; snowflakes are hexagonal, as are the individual lenses in the compound eye of an insect; so is the cross section of a bamboo fly rod. The hexagons of a honeycomb are perfect for their purpose. The surface of the comb is a regular tessellation, that is, one divided into identical geometric shapes that adjoin one another with no gaps or oddly shaped spaces. All the edges meet perfectly—the first design constraint in conserving construction materials. There are only three ways to tessellate a flat surface: with equilateral triangles, with squares, and with hexagons; of these, the hexagon encloses the greatest area with the least perimeter. Thus an array of hexagonal chambers will hold the most honey while requiring the least amount of wax to build, a tremendous advantage since producing wax is a heavy drain on the resources of the hive. From an engineering standpoint, the architecture is equally superb. A hexagonal cell maximizes strength; extremely thin and light, it can hold twenty-five times its own weight, and the wax is recyclable. In a movable-frame hive, the comb is constructed to exacting specifications—4.83 cells to the running inch—tens of thousands of them built without instruction or supervision, and in total darkness.

When I used to fish the reach of water that ran past the beehives, I couldn't, of course, see any of this—the hexagons of comb, the dancing, the bee space—and though bees were coming and going all the time, what stood out most perceptibly was the sound. The wing-beat frequency of a field bee at peak power output, about 240 Hz, produces a distinctive pitch, about the equivalent of B below middle C if the worker bee were a piano. But a colony does not sound like a single bee amplified thousands of times; it generates a much lower pitch, less a buzz than an almost infrasonic hum that indicates, among other things, that the air conditioner is running. On a warm summer day, workers will leave the hive to collect water—I would often see dozens of them at the edge of the bank, drinking—and bring it back to the hive, where they spread it over the comb. A great number of other bees then fan their wings to circulate air, setting up a kind of evaporation-cooling system that prevents the wax from melting in the heat. This collective fanning—what I listened to as I fished—is one of the most soothing sounds in all of nature.

As dairy cows are the visible emblem of spring-creek country, so bees are the aural one, the sound of that border, that middle space where the human world feathers into the natural one, a domesticated place that still encompasses wild things, like trout. The wingbeat of honeybees is the resonant frequency of the landscape, a sound that is as acoustically similar as it is psychologically identical to the sound of moving water.

Bees, like cows, are said to be domesticated, and it is certainly true that they participate in a domestic arrangement. But I doubt that either has the slightest awareness of its own domestication. They simply do what they have always done. Any adjustment or accommodation on behalf of this arrangement must be made by the farmer or apiarist. And when you consider how he provides for and protects, husbands and oversees his charges, it does make you wonder, between the keeper and the kept, exactly who has domesticated whom.

Beekeepers have an expression—"queenright"—that they use to describe a hive. Technically, it refers to a colony with a functioning queen, that is, one that is laying eggs. You may sometimes hear it used, though, in a more metaphorical way, not merely to describe a hive with a queen, but with a good queen, one who produces brood long and steadily, and so maintains a high morale and sense of purpose in the colony, since perpetuation is what every bee in the hive lives for. In this sense, a queenright hive is one in which life is consistent and productive, in which the bees are in good spirits, well-satisfied, and, as Langstroth might have said, "happy." And for five or six seasons, this was precisely how I felt about driftless country, not yet aware that such things can change in an instant.

6

Brothers in Arms

~~~~~~~~~~

The stories we tell ourselves create the very space that we as a

group, any group, inhabit. Place is made by story.

—Michael Martone, *The Flatness and Other Landscapes*

Fishing, as already indicated, was not, like hunting, an

occupation for heroes.

—A. J. B. Wace and F. H. Stubbings, *A Companion to Homer*

Every landscape is really two landscapes. It is first the place that exists when you are not there, unpreconceived, unaltered by perceptions, undisturbed even by words. This version of a landscape is difficult and, perhaps by definition, impossible to know. Attempt to insinuate yourself into its secret life, try to make yourself just as small as possible and sneak a peak, and you inevitably change it. Our understanding of such a place, or what we think we know, comes through inference and extrapolation. You can never truly see a world that doesn't have you in it, though trying to do so, I think, is critically important. Such acts of sympathetic imagination are sometimes powerful enough to stave off chain saws and bulldozers, drilling rigs and high explosives. The unalloyed landscape is what we often seek in nature, even as we know it can never be discovered.

What we find instead is the landscape that exists when we are there, which is at least as much an idea about the place as it is the place itself. The landscape we experience is a highly charged, ionized space that attracts to itself countless particles of association, of past days spent there and events that occurred, of similar places and times, of the people who have shared in them, of a thousand arbitrary details—a smell, a quality of light—that become inseparable from the landscape. In the strange alchemy of memory, such associations consolidate and fuse so tightly together that a place no longer just recalls these things; it becomes them. A landscape builds within us, the sum of its natural and cultural elements, of all that has happened there, of our memories of those things, of the stories we tell about our recollections, of the characters that people those stories. We weave all these threads together on the loom of a landscape, and the word "place" becomes a shorthand for the fabric we make.

Fishing the spring creeks of the driftless area, as I have said, almost always involved a group of us, a constantly shifting collection of neophytes and quasi anglers. While on any given occasion we rarely numbered more than five or six, by the end of a few seasons as many as fifteen or twenty different people had made the trip. I didn't recognize this at the time, but Jerusalem Creek was becoming for me a kind of litmus test. In searching for trout streams, I was also seeking out, or perhaps trying to create, fishing companions, though it mattered little to me how well they fished or how quickly they learned or, odd as it may sound, whether they were interested in fishing at all. Without really being aware of it I was looking to see if they felt some chemistry, a rapport with place that is still the first and best quality in a fishing partner and also the reason that it is not necessary that a good fishing companion actually fishes. The spring creeks were more than just trout streams to me, and I wanted them to be the same for these other people. Only long afterward would I recognize in this desire my first crude attempt to find the sort of community that, in various forms, I have been searching for ever since and in a few rare instances have found, though only once or twice in ways related to trout streams.

The idea of community may seem like fairly heavy freight to load onto something as slight as fishing, and I hesitate even to use the word—not because of its weight, but because the term has been emptied into weightlessness. Its indiscriminate use now runs from the moronic—a new pesticide, for example, poses a risk to the "orange-juice-drinking community"—to the oxymoronic, in something like the "corporate community," whose members, as far as I can see, are united solely by their desire to devour one another. The drift into total paradox is not far off. Media pundits already refer to "the homeless community," and the day some talking head speaks with a straight face about the "hermit community" or the "community of misanthropes," the disappearance of the word into pure nothingness will be complete, another helpless victim of "euphemasia"—the extermination through premeditated misuse, death by euphemism.

Although the notion of community first dawned on me, if only dimly, in the pastoral landscape of spring creeks, I did not discover it in the land itself. To look to the natural world for moral instruction is a dangerous business at best, for much of what you find there is antithetical to the best impulses of human culture. In nature, the strong dominate the weak, charity and sympathy have no place; infanticide, thievery, self-interest, and opportunism are commonplace.

Obviously, these are human categories, which is in a way precisely the point. The dynamics of the natural world are neither evil nor ethical—they are morally unaligned, merely the ongoing adjustments by which things are made to work; they simply are what they are. And what they are must be respected, but not necessarily imitated. Nature is an excellent teacher, but it teaches mostly about itself. Neither did this idea of community arrive in the form of Damascene revelation. It was only the altogether ordinary recognition that other people do not exist merely as adjuncts of yourself, planets orbiting in your own personal solar system; they are separate worlds, with their own atmospheres and life, that might be worth a trip. You begin to understand that communities come in two forms: the ready-made kind that you are born into or join, and the type that you might fashion or negotiate in a way that best accords with your own sense of sustaining connection. In short, you see a potential within the larger world for creating a smaller and perhaps more authentic one. And if this is a thoroughly unremarkable insight into the nature of people, it is still an exciting one, at least at first, and was doubly so for me because I began glimpsing these possibilities in conjunction with a landscape that itself represented to me a kind of independence.

I couldn't blame the others for not sharing this notion, at least insofar as I understood it myself. Everyone joined in these fishing expeditions for somewhat different reasons, and most of them never found spring-creek country, as I did, to be one of those entirely sufficient places. As time went on, the number of participants began to dwindle. For a few, like the Greenberg brothers and Moonrat, the outings turned out to be only a passing lark, one temporary diversion in a life of many. Others never saw what all the fuss was about; it was just a fishing trip, often of a distinctly unproductive type, and they lost interest in returning. A few were not invited back.

Pat, the best fisherman I knew to that point, joined the army, and though I fully expected we'd fish together afterward, somehow we never did. J.B. bought a Ford pickup older than he was and rigged it with a camper nailed together from an old billboard he'd found; he headed west and embarked on a strenuous regimen of self-medication. A few years later, what was left of him returned. Mickey, the first of us to be married, was devoted to his new wife and eager to get out in the world and fished with us only from time to time. Others traveled away to school and stayed away or came back as strangers or just drifted off into lives that did not include a trout stream.

As the number of fishermen slowly grew during the first few seasons, so it gradually diminished during the next few. The ordinary circumstances of living closed in on the edges of this group and summer after summer nibbled away the periphery a bit at a time, until eventually only a handful of us remained, the same few who had started the whole thing, which may well have been destined from the beginning. We were the most serious fishermen of the bunch, and maybe for that reason were more attuned to the landscape and grew more attached to it than the rest. The decline in numbers was a natural attrition, no formal partings or hard feelings, and when it looked to be over, the arrangement that was left suited us fine. There were four of us then, my two brothers and I, and a friend who had somehow become attached to us so long ago that he might as well have shared our blood since he shared nearly everything else. We got along well together, and particularly so when fishing, simply because nothing else seemed possible. I was still naïve enough to believe that it was always this way among brothers, that rivalry or enmity or mutual indifference occurred only outside of families; the world took its time in educating me on this point, though I eventually caught on. We found great pleasure and amusement in one another's company, and by the time the expeditions to driftless country had thinned down to the four of us, we had already evolved the kind of easy routines and dovetailing patterns that make fishing with a good partner as effortless and satisfying as fishing alone. We knew the stretches of streams and types of water that each favored and deferred to those preferences, bypassing choice spots to leave for the others, or summoning the rest to places that were fishing well, indulging one another's idiosyncracies, humoring the foibles and tolerating the bad habits. Close to begin with, we grew closer still through the agency of this place.

As far as I was concerned, one could not want better trout streams than these spring creeks or find better partners to fish them with, and indeed, I regarded them as all of a piece, for a good fishing companion is the human equivalent of home water. You come by them both, people and places, in many of the same ways—a quirk of birth, trial and error, a chance introduction by someone else, an accidental proximity. And you value them both for many of the same reasons— their familiarity and dependability, the small changes from year to year, the capacity for surprise. Each is a landscape, with favorite places and with ones that are best avoided, but a well-known territory to which you always anticipate returning. To bring them together and fish home water with home companions is to inhabit one of the most agreeable of all spaces.

We fished together like this for a season or two, unaware that it would not last, still unacquainted with the precarious impermanence of the world. The death of my youngest brother tore a hole through the heart of this small group, a raw and ragged void, a great empty place surrounded by grief. We rarely spoke of it at first, disbelieving that he would have left us like that, by choice, with no warning, on our own. Later, we talked more, searching for reasons and causes, for a

tale to tell that would accommodate this unspeakable dimin-
ishment, to fix an explanation like a photograph, crisp and
sharp. But our talk served only to apply a balm of words, the
warm compress of story, and perhaps that is all that can
really be done. Words couldn't fill the wordless space, but
they worked upon its jagged edges and slowly knit this
emptiness into the tissue of the landscape. It too became part
of the place, one occupied by a paradox, by something that
isn't there, a hollow space in which drifted the phantom, untold stories of a thousand things that would never happen.
An absence that could reverberate as powerfully as presence
made the landscape both larger and smaller, stranger and
more intimate at the same time. And fishing there became
for a while one of those small acts of defiance that keep you
from disappearing into everyone else, a private revenge that
you mistakenly believe keeps some part of you alive.

From then on, there were just three of us. Although a few
others occasionally fished it with us over the years, spring-
creek country had become distinctly our place, and the map
of the territory, always building in my head, now shaped itself around my two companions.

The first of these was, and still remains, my brother Greg,
though it is strange to use this name or to see it written on
the page, since he has been known to his close friends as
Gecko for the better part of his life. The name refers to nothing reptilian in his nature and, in fact, except for being his
name, signifies nothing at all but the universal propensity
among intimates—families or friends, colleagues or comrades in arms—to evolve a private language; indeed, its very
existence might be taken as a measure of their intimacy. I expect such languages are familiar to all, the words and expres-
sions, the malapropisms and botched punch lines, the allusions
and references that are given meaning by shared experience
and accumulate as part of a communal history. Ours derived

from an almost purely anarchic form of wordplay first devised and most eloquently practiced by my next-door neighbor Mickey. Its governing logic was sound more than sense, its internal dynamic one of continual transmutation. Based on their aural properties alone, ordinary words served as the uranium for uncontrolled linguistic chain reactions that eventually mushroomed into a lexicon which read like a poor man's *Finnegans Wake.* It included bizarre coinages, the truncations or forced marriages of words, and a free insertion of verbal wild cards that probably reached its most cryptic in a horrible honking vocalization, like a cat hacking up a hairball, that performed a variety of functions aside from irritating other people—greeting, farewell, assent, disapproval, and contact call. Most of these utterances were transitory forms with a half-life of moments before they metamorphosed into something else. But some, like "Gecko," came to rest in a stable state, perhaps because the giving of names is a ritual by which a community lays claim to one of its own. Needless to say, "Mickey" was not my neighbor's real name either.

Although the Gecko is two years my junior, people often mistake him for the elder brother—"Because," as he never fails to point out, "I am more mature." We are said to look alike—even strangers occasionally comment on it—but neither of us sees much resemblance. We do have in common some of those secondary traits that often run in families: the same gestures and mannerisms, gait and posture, the same inflections of voice and verbal timing, the same sense of humor. Unlike me, however, he is a frighteningly well adjusted human being, possessing an instinctive capacity to distinguish between small things and large ones, between life's trifles and its matters of consequence, between horseshit and fertilizer—a capacity, I am convinced, that he was born with, for while I haven't known him all my life, I've known him all of his. I have met only a few other people like this, who appear to have arrived in this world somehow whole and self-sufficient, already having negotiated some peace with it, intuiting its rules or understanding themselves sooner or better than the rest of us. Such people are often of a quiet and contemplative manner, the type you'd be least likely to notice in a gathering, but usually the ones most worth knowing. They are content and simply find no real reason to talk a great deal about it. At the same time, they tend to stay somewhat innocent of certain categories of human experience, principally those born of desperate need, since they themselves need little and what they require they have managed to find. The consequence, for my brother, has been an equanimity and surefootedness in the world that make him a great favorite among the people he meets and have made him as well, for as long as I can remember, seem older than his age. I have never known anyone less prey to self-delusion, or indeed delusions of any kind, though no one, of course, is entirely free of them.

He is, as my father was, a physicist by training and an engineer by profession who holds all things up first to the clear and unsentimental light of reason, and examines them with a rigor and relentlessness that can be unnerving at times—when, for instance, he pursues a conversation to the point where you are confronted with the inconsistencies of your own thinking and forced to admit that you do not really know what the hell you are talking about. It's nothing personal; inquisitive and intellectually honest rather than aggressive and tactical, he is far from argumentative—but if you wish to talk serious ideas, he will take you seriously. An orderliness of mind makes him impatient at times with those murkier aspects of human behavior that are inherently irrational and muddled, and these sometimes bring out in him the willfulness of a person who has reason on his side and cannot see why you can't see it. On these occasions, my wife is moved to remind him of a line from a John Sayles movie: "Just because you can argue better doesn't mean you're right." You may also, if infrequently, glimpse a flashing temper like my father's, shorter-lived but ignited by the same things—stubbornness in error, pomposity, selfishness, and ignorance masquerading as knowledge. He has an edge to him, though you might know him a very long time before ever realizing it.

What you sense instead is a gentle and deferential nature (also like my father), a willingness to accept people exactly as they are, and the kind of skepticism that shows itself most often in a wickedly droll sensibility and irreverent ironic wit. He regards "*Homo sapiens*" as the most baffling of taxonomic choices, man as a species to be little more than a chimp with car keys, and the general doings of the world to be predictable but still unbelievable. This is not a philosophy of life but a brand of pragmatism that makes the business of living more workable simply because humankind's endless appetite for folly rarely takes him by surprise. But his is a qualified skepticism; man, in the abstract, alternately amuses and appalls him, but he is devoted to individual people.

An illness during adolescence left him nearly without hearing in one ear, and despite a passion for music, he has taken the loss in stride, even finding certain benefits in it. At night, he lays his good ear against the pillow and turns a deaf ear to the noise of the world, a practice that, perhaps more than anything, suggests his general approach to life. Of shockingly modest wants for a contemporary American, he has chosen his professional circumstances less on the basis of the work or money involved than on the amount of free time that they make available. If you can swing it, this seems to me an eminently reasonable starting point for sane living; and from it, my brother has pretty much struck out on his own path in the belief that true things are where you find them and that reason is not the only or best or even most interesting of life's touchstones. Heart and spirit must satisfy their own ways of knowing, and if the logic of science and that of the soul do not always lead to the same place, physics and metaphysics sometimes share parallel trajectories. In the end, thoughtfulness and mindfulness may prove more alike than different, and to negotiate them is at least worth a try. He serves, for instance, as treasurer of his zendo because it is possible that spiritual practice may one day reveal something worth seeing, but in the meantime even the roshi must eat.

I find him excellent company on a trout stream, and especially on extended trips, where sour weather, poor fishing, car trouble, thwarted hopes or a hundred other misfortunes are never far away. Resourceful and composed, Gecko has many times ballasted my own tendency toward homicidal fantasy. Aside from these things, he is a good hand with a canoe, shoots a fair game of pool, and will try anything once. He lives a life of calculated simplicity, almost monkishly spare in many respects, but is generous, often lavishly so, to others. He ties the deadliest Hare's Ear nymphs that I've ever used, and we have fished together since we were small boys.

Our companion in exploring driftless country was a mutual friend who, for reasons that are best left undisturbed, was called Lizard from the very start. The issue of prolific parents, Lizard entered the world somewhere near the middle of a string of nine children. The dynamics of a large family often operate along Darwinian lines, and unsurprisingly, Lizard developed early on a keen sense of survival, camouflaging himself when prudent and rising to the competition if victory appeared feasible. At the age of seven or so, he adopted my family; took to calling my mother, a woman of somewhat formal manner, "Ma," which both shocked and pleased her; and generally began making himself comfortable in all other regards. He spent much of his time at our house and much of that time maneuvering vast quantities of buttered toast into his open mouth, and I remember him in those days chiefly as an odd species of baby bird. In the end we had little choice but to adopt him in return, an arrangement that has stood unchanged for nearly forty years.

Like other people I've known of a self-assured and independent spirit, Lizard is constitutionally incapable of suffering fools and never shy about saying so. He had no patience with the parochial school we attended as children, and the nuns who taught us regarded him, in the terminology of the day, as something of a "problem child." When his school class arrived at the age of confirmation—a ritual of the Catholic church by which one is formally drafted into the organization—each confirmee was required by tradition to take the name of a saint or biblical figure, a kind of totemic alliance that has probably been a part of human ceremonial rites since the beginning. Lizard announced, to the riotous glee of his classmates, that he had chosen "Lucifer," which fit rather well since he presided over the pandemonium that followed. The belief in himself and the delight in tweaking institutional authority have not abated, though these days he takes a more subversive, beat-them-at-their-own-game approach.

I've known just a few people in my life who possessed what I would call an innate sense of good taste, and Lizard was the first, naturally discerning in books and music, food and wine (he is a gifted cook), and with a particularly discriminating eye when it comes to the visual arts, architecture, and matters of design. He was born, in short, with a nose for quality and appreciates it in all its forms—a thing that is beautiful or eloquent, or perfectly suited to its purpose, or honestly made—whether it be a Kandinsky or a corkscrew. But much like my brother, he is a creature of modest wants, indifferent to possessing the things he admires but valuing the human imagination that they represent. Conversely, he holds deep contempt for anything that, through laziness, deceit, moral failure, or curable ignorance is shoddy, second-rate, or banal. He would walk blocks out of his way to abuse a mime, and exposure to the more egregious forms of American kitsch, like show tunes, practically crushes his will to live. Gecko delights in exploiting this weakness, humming a few bars from something truly dreadful, like *Cats*, in a form of customized torture he calls "the Hamlisch maneuver" and often administers to rein in Lizard's deliberately exaggerated arrogance. This ironic posture, cultivated as a mode of retaliatory persecution, turns on an elaborate self-parody in which a condescending superiority is aired in a taunting, up-yours, Muhammad Ali style. But such are the complex pathologies of long friendship.

Like Gecko, Lizard has made his own way in the world, though for the most part I believe it was a tougher trip, as it typically proves for people who hold unrealistically high standards. In trying to find a meaningful foothold in life, he worked a variety of jobs, some menial, some professional, only to find each eventually declining into its own brand of spirit-snuffing tedium. So at an age when most others have settled comfortably into a career, he cast about for a new life and, to my continuing disbelief, began seeking an academic position under the assumption that, if higher education does not exactly reward innovative ideas and original thinking, it is at least too befuddled to punish them. It's not clear whether he heeded Gecko's parting injunction—"When you go for the interview, Lizard, for God's sake don't be yourself"—but he got the job and is now a professor at a large public university, "a ward of the state, at last," he sighs.

As friends usually do, the three of us shared some common ground, a territory where we saw eye to eye on important matters, and fishing was one of them. Trout streams and the landscapes that contained them registered on us in much the same way, and we held similar ideas about fishing: about how seriously it should be taken, what to invest in it, where its thrills and limits were, why we did it in the first place, and how much was enough. But to say that we were like-minded in this regard is not to say that we fished alike. You fish who you are; you cannot do otherwise. For better or worse, one's personality, life experiences, and general makeup assert themselves indiscriminately, and there is no reason that fishing should be spared. What might be called "heightened states," whether induced by the marvel of modern pharmaceuticals or a jolt of religion or a trout stream, are far less likely to change people into something else than to amplify what is already there. The sentimental drunk, in my experience, is still sentimental when he's sober, and I've never seen a fistful of Valium, a dose of the spirit, or a pool full of rising trout transform an asshole into Mother Teresa. Such things bring out the person you are, and we choose our fishing partners to make the revelation as agreeable as possible.

My brother and I learned to fly fish for trout at roughly the same time and often together, and while we compared notes and showed each other what we'd discovered, we had no precise idea of the how the thing should be done. We proceeded mainly by instinct, each of us more or less making it up as he went along, a process of parallel evolution that allowed each to recreate a version of the sport that best conformed to his nature and inclinations. And we ended up, unsurprisingly, differing as fishermen to precisely the degree we differed as people. Patient and deliberate in all matters, Gecko became a thorough, unhurried fisherman, working his water carefully and completely, sometimes in a way that still makes me fidget, as my own style fits somewhere between the haphazard and the reckless. I have many times left him on the banks of a small creek, returned later, and found he'd moved only a hundred yards from where he'd started in the time I'd gone half a mile. Analytically minded, he reads water well, and this is the aspect of his game I most appreciate. In the logic of planning and economy of movement, he calls to mind a good pool player—always thinking a few moves ahead, efficient but not rushed, knowing that true skill lies not in turning the trick shot but in positioning yourself to make every setup just as straightforward and easy as possible. He is, in short, a systematic fisherman, though this is far different from employing the kind of angling "systems" one finds peddled in magazines and books, those algorithms of fish extraction that begin with programmatic "techniques" and culminate in the vending of flies, leaders, lines, tackle, and videotapes. I am quite familiar with this kind of system; it is called "capitalism." It has produced some wealthy practitioners, but no good fishermen that I'm aware of. All forms of fly angling reward care and persistence, but none more than nymphing, and it is no accident that Gecko is skilled at it. Despite my gentle admonitions over the years, he remains primarily a wrist-caster—the legacy of short-line fishing on tiny creeks—but he makes up in line control what he gives away in distance. He fishes for the strike and cares little about bringing a trout to hand once he's had the chance to see it.

Lizard took up a fly rod a couple of seasons later. As little as I knew about fly fishing, he knew even less and so subjected himself to the tragedy of my instruction. He spent the first few years scrupulously reproducing all my bad habits and the last twenty-five trying to undo them, and while he's succeeded in this to a surprising degree, some of the damage appears permanent. Where Gecko selects his water and fits his methods to it, Lizard is inclined to choose a technique—most often a dry fly, because he prefers it—then seek out trout that share his opinion. A creature of ritual, he begins his day on the water, even at dawn, with a bottle of beer and a cigar, and while moderate in these habits, he nonetheless subscribes to a theory of fully integrated pleasures. With a long-billed cap and thin, sharpish features, he is somewhat heronlike in appearance, and very much so in manner, casting and fishing with an expectant forward lean that makes my back hurt to watch. He does not, thankfully, covet or deserve what seems to be the sport's highest accolade these days—"fly-fishing predator"—nor is he one of those swaggering jocks you sometimes meet on the water who believe it's not only possible but a solemn obligation to catch every trout in the stream. He simply gives fishing his fullest attention. Where Gecko is patient, Lizard is tireless and, if left unchecked, might walk your legs off in a day of fishing. He has quick reflexes, swears under his breath when he misses a strike, and despite a stubborn insistence on a certain level of comfort in almost everything else, is remarkably indifferent to bad weather, bad water, or bad fishing. A few trout satisfy him, though the bigger the better.

As the three of us fished together more, we also began lengthening our stays in spring-creek country, from day trips to weekends to three-day weekends, and finally to those long, vacant weekday stretches that are the best time on any trout stream. Extending our trips meant camping out, a prospect we eyed with both eagerness and misgiving, since none of us had ever camped, nor did we come from families that could be called, even in the most tortured construction of the word, "outdoorsy." My father, in particular, regarded leaving the comforts of hearth and home merely, as he put it, "to eat from paper plates, swat bugs, and sleep on the ground" as a species of madness. And I think for quite a long time, he remained bemused and mildly appalled that his own offspring, creatures who shared half his genetic material, could entertain such an idea with any seriousness. But he never once uttered a critical remark or tried to discourage us. Quite the contrary. He sympathized with the plight of our inexperience as we struggled to equip ourselves, but not being a camper himself, had little to offer in the way of practical counsel. He watched our preparations with interest, puffing on his pipe, and when they were complete, he sincerely bid us to "have a good time," which, as a rational and open-minded man, he conceded was at least theoretically possible. So we learned to camp as we did to fish, by familiarizing ourselves with every error and faulty decision that could be made, though we specialized in two main categories: first, bringing almost nothing we actually needed, like food, drink, flashlights, and something to sit on; and second, carting along instead all manner of pointless camping baggage that was recommended in a Boy Scout manual published half a century earlier—a shovel, for instance (the point of which is still not clear to me); surplus wooden army cots; and a double-mantle white-gas lantern that blazed like a supernova yet somehow failed to shed a single photon of usable light.

The one piece of marginally functional gear that we owned was an old-style canvas cabin tent. We had obtained it for next to nothing and, as Huck Finn once said, "It was worth it, too." I still cannot summon to mind the splendid landscape of Jerusalem Creek without conjuring up as well an image of that dismal edifice. It was, for starters, gargantuan. Neatly folded and rolled, the canvas alone took up most of the back of a station wagon, and the poles took up the rest; it required two of us to lift from the car and three of us half a morning to set up. Even when brand-new, it projected a kind of architectural ennui, a world-weary sag that no amount of rope tightening or pole adjusting could eliminate, and Lord knows we tried, since keeping the thing upright at all demanded perpetual vigilance. And though the bright blue walls and sunshine yellow roof took a failed stab at cheerfulness, like a concession tent at a cheap carnival where vaguely menacing men dispense corn dogs, it was an imposing structure still.

Unless you happened to camp on a putting green, you were unlikely to find an expanse of level, smooth acreage large enough for this Taj Mahal. Wherever it was spread out, the tent floor acquired its own complex topography, and each night at bedtime, you chose whether to sleep in the mountains or in the valleys or, if the weather turned bad, in the riverbeds. Despite two full-width windows and a double-size screened door, not the slightest breeze stirred inside on even the windiest days. The resulting cube of stagnant air functioned as a thermal reservoir large enough to generate its own weather. On pleasantly mild days, our tent steamed inside like a Turkish bath; as the night air cooled, clouds formed near the ceiling, and in the morning, you wandered through a fetid, malarial fog to find the door. It was waterproof only in the sense that falling rain did not directly strike your person; it was first absorbed, in unimaginable quantities, by the massive canvas shell. But once the fabric became saturated, each raindrop hitting the roof or walls propelled an equal volume of tiny water droplets down inside the tent, creating a mist that fell so gently you never woke until soaked to the skin. When the sun returned, the walls sprouted a vigorous fuzz, and after only a few trips, its merry hues were permanently blotched and mottled by thriving colonies of single-celled animals.

We spent little time inside the tent anyway, finding the open air more salubrious even in foul weather, and some nights we threw a sleeping bag on the grass and slept outside, though it never once occurred to us just to leave the tent at home. By custom, we pitched this behemoth at a spot on the upper, mostly fishless, section of Jerusalem Creek, and so spent little time at camp anyway, driving downstream in the morning, or off to other creeks, or out scouting, returning only in late afternoon after we'd fished ourselves to exhaustion. On the way back, we collected firewood, which usually involved climbing up a roadside slope, cutting down a dead tree, and tethering it to the car bumper with a length of rope. I drove slowly down the road while Lizard and Gecko walked behind, picking up kindling-size branches that snapped off against the pavement. By the time we reached camp, the peeled and limbless trunk was ready for sawing into campfire lengths. Except for the dragging part, which was our own invention, this process of felling a tree and bucking it into fire logs is regionally known as "making wood," and every afternoon we made enough to stoke a small iron smelter.

The predictable result was, in that well-known Native American phrase, a "white man's fire," a fuel-intensive conflagration several orders of magnitude larger than required for any practical purpose. While we did cook dinner over the fire—we believed this was required in camping—its chief function was recreational, and to that end I suppose there's really no such thing as a campfire that's too big. Invariably, Gecko engineered and tended these flame balls, for though a streak of pyromania ran deep in us all, he brought to bear a singular gift for the architectonics of combustion and draft management, and always produced a stylish fire. I saw him fail only once, and that not many years ago, on a rainy evening with sodden and inferior materials; his disappointment turned to humiliation when my wife, innocent of campsite protocol and seeking only to help, stepped in and kindled a serviceable blaze with a handful of Kleenex scavenged from her purse. My brother has never quite recovered from this.

In the end, sitting around the fire proved to be the one part of camping we were any good at, and so we devoted considerable time to it. Applying the torch before sundown, we fed the campfire steadily throughout the evening, periodically consulting the cooler to fish a beer from the confusion of apples and gutted trout and slimy yogurt cups that bobbed together in a slosh of tepid water. On clear nights, when the fire burned low and the Milky Way glowed above like a band of creamy fog, we leaned back and studied the sky, finding the few constellations we knew, wondering why they'd been given the names that so little resembled them.

"You know, Lizard," Gecko would say, gazing up wistfully, "looking at all those millions of stars makes me realize how insignificant you really are."

Lizard, unmoved, would lift a bony haunch and crack a short burst of contempt.

〰〰〰〰〰

For a while, there would be talk of the day, of the water we'd worked and what we'd seen, trout caught or not, and from there, on to talk of other times and places we had been, and rivers we hoped to fish someday, and how strange it would seem then for there to be only three of us. We carpentered this talk into stories and added them to others already told and to the untold stories of a thousand things that would never happen, and arranged them all at the edge of the firelight, creating this place within a place. Eventually, the conversation thinned out in the cool air and words vanished beneath the canopy of a lampblack sky pierced with stars. From time to time, we stayed up until the last flames died out and the red-orange coals crumbled to lightless ash in the fire ring, and still we waited, reluctant to leave even this scorched and empty circle, this scar branded into the skin of the land. For at its heart were those wordless things that make all our stories lies.

7

Certain Specific Days

~~~~~~~~~~~

I heard the old, old men say,

"Everything alters,

And one by one we drop away."

They had hands like claws, and their knees

Were twisted like the old thorn-trees

By the waters.

I heard the old, old men say,

"All that's beautiful drifts away

Like the waters."

—W. B. Yeats, "The Old Men Admiring Themselves in the Water"

For a time there was a photograph, a 35mm slide to be precise, that was taken on Jerusalem Creek, and though it is gone now, I can still summon its details to mind with a near perfect vividness. In the center of the frame is a fisherman, still a few years shy of twenty, standing with the forced nonchalance of a person who poses reluctantly—narrow hips cocked to shift his weight to the right leg, left knee bent a little, right hand in his pocket. His shoes, which have just made it into the bottom of the picture, are muddy, and you can tell from the abrupt change to dark blue that his faded jeans are wet to the thighs. He is wearing a flannel shirt, red and black checked, out at the elbows, the too long sleeves rolled up at the cuffs. Two buttons are missing from the front; you cannot see it in the picture, but I know because the shirt once belonged to me, and was then on its last stop in a succession of hand-me-downs. A rolled bandanna, red as the king of hearts and knotted around the forehead, holds back his dark hair, left uncut to grow past his shoulders, a streak of blood-red against tanned skin. His left arm is raised and partially extended, blue veins clearly visible on the underside of his forearm, black watchband on the wrist. Suspended by two fingers, from the underside of its jaw, is a brown trout, a nice fish, a native. It is gutted and the gills removed so that the blood-rich tissue will not spoil in the warm air and taint the meat. The weight of its body, hanging, opens an empty crescent where the gills once were. The fisherman is not looking at the trout or at the camera, but at some point between and beyond them both. His head is turned slightly, casting a faint shadow over the left side of his face that makes his expression distant and unreadable. He has my father's eyes, but I do not know what he is seeing.

I used to look at this picture a great deal. It never appeared to me, as photographs are sometimes described, as a "moment frozen in time." Rather it seemed something sliced and stolen from time, like a single frame clipped from a reel of movie film, a cross section of ongoingness too thin to be missed by anyone, a pellicle of color one-thousandth of a second thick shaved by the microtome of a camera shutter and mounted in a cardboard frame. Held up to a window against the sun, a frame within a frame, it captured a light born ninety-three million miles away, already nine minutes old when it reached me, the incandescence of a thing that once existed lit by an event that has already occurred, the past illuminating the past. The image was written in layers, a laminar record like the limestone hills or like memory, the successive skins of emulsion laid one over another, each crystallizing a single color into a stratum of fossilized light. What story it told, like many stories, took form through accretion; it was built up layer by layer, and out of the accumulation came new and unexpected things, not originally laid down and present by themselves, but brought into being by superimposition, the way red light laid on green gives birth to yellow. What gradually emerged were hue and value, sharpness and blur, depth and perspective, the illusion of life. It wasn't the whole story because there is no such thing, only an 840-square-millimeter pane of what held together after the rest washed away.

There was a time in my life, a span of perhaps three or four years, when my mailing address was a moving target and I lived in a series of rooms and apartments and houses, each only briefly, and somewhere in the chaos and shuffle of these ongoing relocations I discovered one day that the picture was gone. It seems impossible to me now that I could have lost a thing that meant so much. I asked myself over and over how I could have been so careless, so remiss; what I should have done to look after it; how it could be that what we value most is always on the brink of disappearing and we don't even know it. But by then it was too late, and what rushed in to fill the space of absence were sadness and self-reproach and regret, and all the after-the-fact grabbings at empty air that come to one who has a left a treasure unguarded. Until then, I did not really know how a thing made of light could weigh so much. And what I could once touch with my hand and see with my eyes is now only the image of an image in my memory.

If you could see this picture, the leafiness of the trees in the background, the height of the grasses, the flowers in bloom, you might judge the season to be late May, though it is in fact almost the middle of June, and while it is odd, perhaps, that I do not recall the exact year that the photograph was taken, I remember the occasion quite clearly. There are certain rare days unlike all the rest. They begin with no discernible moment of dawn, no perceptible sunrise; a clouded sky merely lightens by degrees, dissolving away the night, and by early morning, it is already as bright as it will become all day. The overcast isn't uniform but a dozen kinds of gray, a marbling of duns, smudges of ash, shades of charcoal blending in and out of one another like a piece of smoky quartz. A low, thick sky muffles the sun and sifts the light; the illumination is indirect and soft, with no apparent origin, a crepuscular light neither bright nor dim filtering down from everywhere at once and resting like a blanket on the land. Shadows are faint and contrasts low, and the scene might strike you as dull or flat were it not for the sumptuous greens of almost preternatural depth. This is not an illusion but a quality of light. Reflected and refracted, absorbed and dispersed by tiny droplets of water in the moisture-laden clouds, the white light of the sun is changed, and the spectral balance tips toward the blue-green. Under such a sky, bright colors, the reds and yellows, are muted and tinged with gray, but greens are drawn to the foreground, full-toned and fiercely rich. Every shade, even the palest ones of young grass shoots and new leaves on a walnut tree, grow darker in tone and deeper in value; their colors appear somehow purer. Subtle gradations in hue emerge with striking clarity, and the hundred greens of a sunny day become a palette of thousands in this extraordinary light. Each leaf and stalk and vine stands out with a singular sharpness and heightened definition; every detail is enhanced in resolution and dimension, etched more deeply in texture and relief. Color piles upon color in a concentration of green that supersaturates the landscape with such intensity that you begin to suspect there is something different about your eyes. This, too, is no illusion. Perhaps as a legacy from our arboreal ancestors, human vision is most sensitive to shades of green, keenly attuned to their detection and differentiation. On certain days, the landscape and the eye meet in a harmony that is essentially biological, both lured outward by a light that seems a substance mixed in the atmosphere, suffusive and directionless as humid air.

Such light produces no luster or brilliance, no sparks of sun or looming shadows, no ready point of focus, and I believe that a painter would find this kind of day impossible to put on canvas. I did try to take its picture once, to steal a small pane of that phantom light and fix it forever. But I managed only an imperfect simulation, a fugitive expression beneath a red bandanna, against a depthless background of deep green. It was not the thing itself, only a reminder of the thing, a crude chromatic armature to be fleshed out by memory, like the first few notes of a piece of music you already know by heart. A better photographer might well have done more, but not even the best could capture the overwhelming stillness of these certain days, for light alone does not explain them. There is no wind, not the slightest stirring. The moist air, neither hot nor cool, hovers so close to skin temperature that you cannot feel it on your arms or face. Sound travels with abnormal clarity through the dampness, but there is little to hear. The birds are strangely silent on such days. In the overcast, nectar will not rise to the blossoms of wildflowers, and the bees do not work. Even the sun seems still, its arc through the sky obscured by clouds and the diffusion of light so complete that from morning to evening the illumination remains perfectly uniform.

Without the shifting of light and the growing or shrinking of shadows, without the sway of trees in the wind or the swish of grasses, without movement or change, without any "events," as the physicist would say, that mark interval or duration, time slips into neutral and idles there and ceases to give any sense of elapsing. You do not pass such a day; you occupy it, the only animate point in a scene of stasis, like moving through a photograph or being invisible. There is only the water at hand, and all time is now, an indefinite present extending outward equally in all directions. You might fish through such a day in hyperacute awareness of your spatial surroundings while being lost to any temporal ones, until some reflex or instinct or just the dimming of light at dusk taps you on the brain and brings you back at last. And then it occurs to you that you have no idea at all what the hour is or how many have gone by or even when the question last crossed your mind. There is an angling maxim, one I have seen attributed to everyone from Confucius to Herbert Hoover, that claims the hours spent fishing are not deducted from one's allotted span of life on earth. And though I put no stock in the sentiment, as with many adages the truth resides less in the statement than in the perception that gave rise to it, and I suspect that this sense of being located outside time is familiar in some form to nearly everyone who has ever fished.

All passions in life, I think, possess this capacity; it may indeed be how passion is defined, as that which transports us outside of ourselves and envelops us in a kind of perpetual present. But even this transformative quality does not alone explain these certain days. They exist beyond the spell of fishing, beyond the drape of gray-green light, beyond the fold of stillness; or rather, they exist as a convergence of them all into a whole more potent than the sum of its parts, a solvent so powerful that you can vanish into it. The experience is not so much one of engagement, in fishing or in the landscape, but of being somehow absorbed by both. The well-patrolled borders of the self—those keepers of time—dissolve, and whatever is identifiably you goes with them. And though there are moments in fly fishing that may approach the mystical, this is not one of them, for nothing lies beyond it. There are no flashes of illumination, no ecstatic revelations, no glimpses of cosmic oneness, but something quite close to the opposite—a kind of temporary annihilation, more nearly an animal experience than a transcendent one. It feels neither good nor bad; it feels, in fact, like nothing at all, because no one is there to feel it. Whatever emotional or spiritual valence it acquires—renewal or sufficiency, contentment or intimacy—is something you attach to it only afterward, a story you invent to make sense of this . . . what? time suspended? this place outside yourself? this dream awake? . . . I do not know the name for it. And it might very well be some deception, a sleight of hand played by the mind or senses, were it not for that instant, just as the clock starts again, when for a brief moment you remember the relief of a full-body forgetting. And this is the most remarkable part of it all.

But sometimes and more rarely, it does not happen this way. On certain specific days this feeling of unfeeling yields to something else, a sense that creeps in, or has perhaps never left, born in the small, reluctant chamber of the heart that harbors dread, that from experience knows that nothing lasts. Outwardly, everything remains unchanged, the hushed light and soundless air. But a kind of abstraction grows within, some detached part of yourself that watches the rest of you move through the world as though it were someone else. The stillness of an indefinite present gives way to the stillness between the ticking seconds on a clock. Time is no longer suspended but postponed, not stopped but holding its breath. Some unspecified thing feels poised on the edge of happening, faintly familiar as though you've felt it before, but too indistinct to make out, too diffuse in this light to evoke either anticipation or apprehension, just the vague uncertainty of a distant impending. Then comes a point, perhaps late in the afternoon, when without warning a peal of thunder splinters the stillness like a shotgun blast, and you realize at once that all day long, in some place on the underside of consciousness, you have been waiting for rain, for that moment when time starts again and everything will be somehow different, though what it might be you cannot tell from any photograph.

8

The Heart of the Heartland

≈≈≈≈≈≈≈≈≈

Our eyes register the light of dead stars.

—André Schwarz-Bart, *The Last of the Just*

When I was about eleven, I be-
friended a classmate in school, Mike, who turned out to be
the first of a small handful of kindred spirits who would pass
through my life, as I think they do most lives, people who are
important for different reasons at different times. It was clear
from the start that my friend wielded a formidable intellect,
a resourceful imagination, the ability to educate himself to
almost anything, and the will to do so. Such qualities are unusual enough among people generally; in a child, they can be
a little frightening. Mix them with a curiosity that veers to-

ward the fiendish and a determination to satisfy it, and the whole package can get a bit dangerous. In short, I found him an interesting and excellent companion and game as they come. He was and remains a good friend, and though he eventually became an appeals attorney, I cannot hold even that against him.

We convened almost daily in the leisure of après-school hours to indulge our various and wide-ranging mutual pursuits, though we gravitated most often to a couple of particular interests: first, any device that was designed, or could be made, to launch a projectile, which included but was not limited to bows and crossbows, air rifles, slingshots, cannons fueled by calcium carbide, rockets, and homemade replicas of medieval catapults; and second, any matter involving extremely high heat but especially those terminating in explosions. And an exploding projectile . . . well, there could not be a better world. It was, as you might well imagine, thirsty work, and our enterprises invariably commenced with an after-school snack. Having no children of my own, I do not know if this institution has survived into the contemporary world, though children being what they are, I suspect it has. In my own house, the after-school snack occupied a peculiar and narrow ground, bounded on one side by a list of things forbidden and on the other by a dearth of any suitable substitutes. In that space between what you could not have and what there was, you rarely found room to maneuver, and the snack ordinarily consisted of a desultory scavenge through the refrigerator that generally turned up little more than an apple, a few carrots, or other such disappointments that would not "spoil our dinner." Even then I regarded it as a kind of middle-class Dumpster diving. But at Mike's house, the after-school snack was conducted with all the ceremony of a ritual banquet laid before warriors returned from battle; the board was spread with trenchers of potato chips, wooden bowls of warm popcorn, great tankards of soda, and other of the delicacies that were rationed out at my own house like federally controlled substances. And all of this was cheerfully set before us by Mike's mother, a thin woman with a wide smile and a laugh full of music.

We rarely fell to this feast alone but had in our company Mike's younger brother Patrick, whom, in the grand tradition of older boys, we regarded as the severest form of pestilence, and the still younger Sarah, a blond wisp of American pixiehood with a Buster Brown haircut and miniature voice. One afternoon, in the midst of this group feedbag, Patrick straightened up in his chair and, with the magisterial manner of all children who bear weighty news, announced in a spray of potato-chip crumbs, "Sarah's got a hole in her heart." He paused here for effect. I looked at Sarah who nodded vigorously up and down and grinned so broadly that her eyes closed. After an interval of calculated suspense, he concluded triumphantly, "The doctor's going to plug it with a silver cord!"

I recall the words exactly because I puzzled over them for days. The anatomical details didn't bother me. At the time, I considered myself something of a man of science, had seen illustrations of the organ in question, and had acquired some rudimentary grasp of its operations. Nor was I uneasy about the surgical procedure. I envisioned the silver cord as a scaled-down version of the stranded-steel cable that I used to lock up my bike; how it might be used to "plug" something was not altogether clear, but with unqualified confidence in modern medicine, I assumed that the doctors had worked it all out. What troubled me was one lingering question: how can you even live with a hole in your heart?

This, I discovered much later, was something you had to learn.

There is a particular physiological condition that has been acknowledged in folk wisdom for centuries, but that received its first detailed medical description only in 1871. The Civil War had ended just a few years before and, besides being one of the more thoroughgoing bloodbaths in human history, occurred at a time when prevailing medical practice was still primitive enough to favor amputation as a treatment for battlefield wounds and just sophisticated enough so that for the first time in history a fair portion of the patients survived it. In the years after the war, a neurologist studying these wounded veterans set down the first scientific account of what he termed "sensory ghosts" but has since come to be called "phantom pain"—that phenomenon in which a patient still feels a missing limb to be present and registering sensation, often an excruciating agony. It is a cruel misnomer, since the suffering itself is anything but phantom. It is not the pain of losing—that is separate and real—but the pain of loss, life's double cheat that after the anguish of forfeiture should come the ache of absence. Phantom pain is something brought into being out of the fact of nothingness, the way an image cut from the center of a photograph implies the subject in empty outline. There is stimulation but no stimulus, like closing your eyes in a darkened room and finding in the space behind your lids not blackness but explosions of grainy color—there is no light but still you see, a kind of reverse vision that originates in the mind; or it is like a nightmare when your senses are shut down, dead to the world, but the fear you feel is real. In the aftermath of loss, that part of the brain devoted to a thing now gone fleshes out the empty space, desperate to fill this cavity in the world with feeling, and the missing extremity, that phantom extension of yourself, your own blood and bone, still haunts you. Scarring, but not yet scarred, the mind struggles to reinvest this shell of nothing with the sensation of life, but outwits itself, succeeding all too well, for pain is the only raw material from which to reconstruct that which is gone.

~~~~~~~~~

How can you feel a thing because it is not there? What is it that will not let go but not let you go on, that grips with the unbearable thought of an unbearable future? Why is it that you are one day startled by the perfect ordinariness, the cliché of your own sorrow, as though the well-worn path of grief were not the commonest on earth?

How is it, too, that some people drown where there is no water, sink and suffocate in a life with no oxygen? How is it that they form no scars, no thickened skin that is padding against the world, none of the fibrous, nerveless tissue that allows us to live at all? What mystery of mind or heart makes them feel more keenly rather than less and renders them unable to cast out those demons that inhabit us all? Why do they walk out into the storm clothed only in few millimeters of flesh, the thin suit of their own skins? How much undifferentiated pain must accumulate before they decide to flee this vale of tears? If life is suffering, as all holy men have said, what end is served by the invention of a creature that can die of its own misery?

~~~~~~~~~

On a day in late August, a few valleys to the east of Jerusalem Creek, Gecko and I made a plan to follow a small brook upstream, fishing if it looked promising, just walking if it didn't, but resolved in either event to find the spring from which it issued. I don't recall if we had any reason other than some desire to discover the first source of it, to follow the fisherman's natural impulse to move upstream, an inclination that leads

you one day to take the matter as far it will go, to find the beginning of the thing and get a sense once and for all of the
whole story. We chose a stream we'd fished before, though
not for a few seasons, partly to revisit an old place and partly
because the lay of the land held out some hope for success.
There were no tributaries to divide our attention, and the
creek, though short, had a strong flow that promised a source
of some volume. In the lower reaches at least, the valley was
open and the character of the water familiar; and though upstream the creek wound back to a wooded crease deep in the
ridge and the walking would be tougher, this was the nature
of most of the streams in driftless country.

The summer was nearly over, and the meadow plants
had just topped the crest of ripeness into overripeness, the
headlong momentum of their vigorous growth proving at last
unsustainable. The landscape was a candle alight at both
ends, and the first signs of dying were beginning to appear—
the rich, pure greens now showing the faintest intrusion of
yellow, a few leaves already mottled and fringed in brown.
About halfway down the valley, a bend in the stream swung
close to the road; we parked and walked a short stretch of
meadow to the water. By tacit agreement, there would be no
bypassing around oxbows, no striking a beeline cross-country
to gain ground, no shortcuts; we would follow the stream and
scrupulously track its convolutions until we arrived at the
point where it started. I'm not sure we knew even then what
we wanted or hoped to find, perhaps a rock-rimmed pool secluded in some primeval glade, the water cold and pure and
diamond-clear, concealed from all but those who made the
effort of discovery. Maybe we would be the first to lay eyes
on it.

We walked and walked, for the better part of an afternoon. But in the end there was no mother lode, no defined
and bounded point where we could say, "Here is where it be-

gins; here is the cause of it all." The stream only grew smaller bit by bit, its flow the product of apparently source-less, imperceptible accumulation. We found a few places where water seeped in from the land or trickled up from a patch of sand into the stream, but not enough to account for much, and we must have passed by, unknowingly, a thousand invisible others that only gradually added up to make the stream into the thing that it became. And all of them were merely the outcomes of other unseen origins, underground or up in the hills, with their own causes farther away in distant aquifers and thunderstorms of years ago. There was no whole of it you could grasp at once, not even a beginning to the story. It stretched outward and down and back in all directions at once, beyond explanation or accounting for, because in the end there are no stories but the ones we make.

Later, we pitched camp at our accustomed spot on Jerusalem Creek, and that night Lizard joined us.

At sunrise, you could tell already that the day would be oppressive. August in driftless country can be like this; overnight, damp air pools up in the small valleys, and by morning it thickens to a film of ground fog so dense that you can wring it like a sponge. I found the coffeepot and went off to get water; in the distance, my companions moved noise-lessly about camp, disembodied head and shoulders drifting above a layer of thick, wet smoke. After a while, we headed downstream, and the walk through a dew-soaked meadow to the water left us drenched. In a few hours, a blistering sun would burn away the mist, boiling it to a vapor so hot and steamy that you broke a sweat just breathing, and we would not dry off all day. August can be like this.

At first we worked the usual stretches of Jerusalem Creek, the water we knew best. Under a bright sky in the growing heat, it was a relief to wade wet, though I don't think we caught much, maybe nothing at all. Ordinarily, we would have looked somewhere else, for a colder stream or one with more shade. But no one suggested moving on; there was some shared but unspoken reluctance to leave this familiar place, to let it go on the last trip of a season already waning. So we stayed, though whether we fished more that afternoon, or returned to camp for a while, or merely hunted up a shady spot to escape the listless heat, I don't recall. That entire day exists for me only in discrete fragments, snapshot images and brief scenes, and though memory has tried, as it always will, to stitch and graft these into order, I still see the seams and gaps, and the day has no more coherence than a dream. But I do recall, distinctly, that early evening found the three of us on a reach of the stream we hadn't fished for quite some time. It was exacting water, unusually clear over a sandy bottom, small but deceptively deep, and perhaps its difficulty in earlier years steered us to easier places.

We fished that evening, as we often did, by alternating the new water. We worked short, adjacent sections of the creek, and whoever finished first walked a few bends upstream of the others and put in at a fresh spot. It was a loose arrangement, and some places got inadvertently passed by and others fished twice, but it suited those times when you wished to stay close but still be alone. Just before dusk I was wading up to a small pool formed by a sharp right-angle turn in the creek when I saw the ripples of a good rise spreading slowly outward from somewhere in the corner. I decided to wait and let the trout come up again so I could better mark its location and, in the meantime, try to figure out exactly how I might get a fly back in there. Lizard came walking up from downstream and sat on the bank with me for a while, watching for the trout, and when it did not rise again after a quarter of an hour, he moved on.

What happened next is something I do not so much remember as feel again when I think back to it. After Lizard left, it occurred to me that I hadn't seen Gecko for a while; he hadn't passed me in the meadow, and though it was possible I'd missed him, it didn't seem likely. In a matter of minutes and in a way that I could not account for then, though I believe I can now, my curiosity about where he was darkened to worry, and the worry deepened to an undefined but consuming uneasiness. I abruptly quit fishing and started downstream to the spot I'd last seen him. He was not there—*shouldn't*, I well knew, have still been there—but I was utterly powerless to halt the irrational waves of dread that began to sweep through me. I grew frantic and started walking faster, almost running, shouting for him, and stopping every few moments to listen for a reply. And in each interval of silence, I could feel the panic rising in my throat, could hear it mounting in my voice as I called. I broke into a run, and in the dimming light and tangles of tall grass, stumbled and fell, gashing a knee that was already a candidate for surgery. I got up and began running again, the whole time helplessly watching myself, from somewhere inside, succumb to the power of this inexplicable and overwhelming hysteria.

Then I saw him. He was kneeling at the edge of the water down on the opposite bank, partly hidden behind the bankside vegetation, quietly working a quiet run, his slow, measured casts unfolding over the surface. He hadn't seen me, and I stopped, then sat down, dripping in sweat, my heart still racing, pulse pounding in my ears, blood leaking from my knee. I was suddenly exhausted. I lit a cigarette and watched him for many minutes, calming as the surge of a strange terror drained away. Then I stood and walked to the edge of the bank, catching his eye at last. He said nothing, just raised his head, and I waved him up. He waded across the narrow channel, climbed from the water and into the twilight as the last red of sunset bled eastward to the indigo bruise of an evening sky.

We kept a campfire going late into the night, though it was far too warm for one, and we sat at a distance, just inside the dome of firelight, just within the reach of a heat that dried the humid air. I don't recall that we talked much; there did not seem much to say, each of us treading the dark water of his own thoughts. There must have been no moon, for the stars appeared unusually bright and densely massed in the sky, their numbers, though, only an illusion. Some of them were already gone, consumed by their own intensity, dying long before the first human being ever lived and leaving only the remnant of this sourceless, phantom light that would itself one night simply vanish.

Sometime after midnight, in the small hours of the morning, we rolled out the sleeping bags and turned in. Beyond exhaustion, I lay awake for a while, tossing and restless in the heavy air, and drifted finally into a fitful sleep, dreaming of my mother dreaming of her only sons.

"We are not made," I hear her say, "to bury our children," but I cannot tell in whose dream she speaks.

9

Some Assembly Required

≈≈≈≈≈≈≈≈

What is it that keeps us from drowning in

moments that rise and cover the heart?

—**Anne Carson, "Kinds of Water"**

An old and excellent question.

1. Pharmacopoeia

Here begynnyth a new mater the which sheweth and treateth

of ye virtues & proprytes of herbes.

—*Banckes's Herbal,* **1525**

Hereby, a sort of "cloudiness" will arise from the heart, and envelop the heart in darkness. This is how humans become sad. . . . Take licorice, five times as much fennel seeds, sugar with the same weight as the licorice, and a little honey. Prepare a drink out of these ingredients, and drink for heart pain.

—Hildegard of Bingen, *Causae et Curae,* c. 1150

The black graines (that is the seed [of the peony]) to the number of fifteene taken in wine or mead . . . is a speciall remedie for those that are troubled in the night with the disease called *Ephialtes* or night Mare, which is as though a heauy burthen were laid vpon them, and they oppressed therewith, as if they were ouercome by their enemies, or ouerprest with some great weight or burthen. . . .

The Later writers, among whom *Simeon Zethy* is one, doe teach, that the smell of Basill is good for the heart and for the head. That the seede cureth the infirmities of the heart, taketh away sorrowfulnesse which commeth of melancholy, and maketh a man merry and glad.

—John Gerard, *The Herball, or Generall Historie of Plantes,* 1597

The Scythians, as I said, take some of this hemp-seed, and, creeping under the felt coverings, throw it upon red-hot stones; immediately it smokes, and gives out such a vapor as no Grecian vapor-bath can exceed; the Scyths, delighted, shout for joy.

Herodotus, *Histories IV,* 450 B.C.

For him whose heart pains him . . . take the plant *nonochton* that grows near an ants' nest, gold, electrum, *teoxihuitl, chichiltic tapachtli* and *tetlahuitl,* with the burned heart of a deer, and grind them up together in water; let him drink the liquor.

—Martin de la Cruz, *Libellus de medicinalibus indorum herbis: Manuscrito Azteca de 1552*

The leaves floures and seedes [of borage] are very cordiall
and helpe to expell pensiveness and melancholie.

John Parkinson, *Theatrum Botanicum*, 1640

Ye seed of the black Poppy beaten small is given to drink
with wine. . . . A little of it taken as much as a grain of
Ervum, is a pain-easer & a sleep causer.

—*The Greek Herbal of Dioscorides, c.* second century

Balm

The Arabian physicians have extolled the virtues
thereof to the skies; although the Greeks thought it not
worth mentioning. Seraphio saith, It causes the mind and
heart to become merry, and reviveth the heart, faintings
and swoonings, especially of such who are overtaken in
sleep, and driveth away all troublesome cares and thoughts
out of the mind, arising from melancholy or black choler.

—Nicholas Culpepper, *The English Physician, or An
Astrologo-physical Discourse of the Vulgar
Herbs of this Nation*, 1652

Greek Valerian

It helps in . . . head-achs, trembling, palpitations of
the heart, vapours, and all that train of miserable disor-
ders, included under the name nervous.

—Nicholas Culpepper, *The English Physician, or An
Astrologo-physical Discourse of the Vulgar
Herbs of this Nation*, 1652

A Serecloath for all Aches

Take *Rossen* one pound, *Perrossen* a quarter of a
pound, as *Mastick* and *Deer sewet* the like, *Turpentine*
two ounce, *Cloves* bruised, one ounce, *Mace* bruised,

two ounces, *Saffron* two drams, boyle all these together in Oyle of *Cammomile*, and keep it for your use.

—*A Book of Fruits and Flowers. Shewing The Nature and Use of them, either as Meat or Medicine*, 1653

Roses

Nature: (According to Johannes), cold in the first degree, dry in the third. *Optimum*: The fresh ones from Suri and Persia. *Usefulness*: Good for inflamed brains.

—*Tacuinum Sanitatis*, c. 1400

Apium is good for lunatyke Folke yf it be bounde to the pacyentes heed with a lynen clothe dyed reed.

—*Grete Herball*, 1526

Wine . . . maketh glad the heart of man.

Psalm 104:15

In like sort the rest of the Indians for their pastime do take the smoke of the Tabaco, to make themselves drunke withall, and to see the visions, and things that represent unto them, that wherein they do delight.

—Nicholas Monardes, *Ioyfull Newes ovt of the newe founde worlde, wherein is declared the rare and singular vertues of diuerse and sundrie Hearbes*, 1577

To make a bath for Melancholy. Take Mallowes, pellitory of the wall, of each three handfulls; Camomel flowers, Mellilot flowers, of each one handfull; hollyhocks, two handfulls; Isop one great handfull, senerick seede one ounce, and boil them in nine gallons of Water untill they come to three, then put in a quart of new milke and go into it bloud warme or something warmer.

—Mary Fairfax, manuscript, c. 1632

If they drynk this drynke [mandrake wine] they shall fele no payne, but they shall fall into a forgetfull and slepishe drowsiness.

—William Turner, *The first and second partes of the Herbal of William Turner Doctor in Phisick lately oursene corrected and enlarged with the Thirde parte*, 1568

2. Lethe

Life must go on;

I forget just why

—Edna St. Vincent Millay, "Lament"

As the inheritors of over a century's worth of thought in evolutionary biology, we accept more or less without question that the ability to learn, to remember experience and shape behavior around those recollections—that is, to bring the past into the present—is a successful adaptation for survival. It's hard to argue with this. The individual animal that can, through whatever genetic anomaly, remember sooner or more reliably than the others where it found food at a particular season of the year, or remember the smell of an enemy or the boundaries of its home territory, has a better chance of surviving and passing on that trait to its children, and they to their own children, until it is no longer a genetic idiosyncrasy but standard equipment for the species. So highly, in fact, do we regard this capacity to remember that we not only recognize its evolutionary utility but use it as a gauge; we consider species that learn more, or more readily, to be more advanced or sophisticated. A dog that can distinguish the face and voice of its owner, that can be trained to herd sheep or retrieve ducks is to us a more estimable creature than a rat, whose memory pretty much peaks at running a maze. We construct hierarchies based on feats of recall, and the creatures that remember more are placed closer to the top of the pyramid for the simple and unsurprising reason that they more nearly resemble us.

But, perhaps paradoxically, as the faculty of memory develops and grows more extensive in reach, there comes a point where the capacity to forget, which we most often deem a failing, in fact represents an equally crucial mechanism for survival. I can't prove this, but only point to the fact that some small part of the complex circuits of memory seem already wired for forgetting. There is a kind of time decay in the emotional or psychological capacitance of a charged experience, a slow leakage of current, a gradual ramping down of voltage, so that in time you might handle the thing without getting electrocuted. You can call it an inefficiency, a loss of resolution, a failure of integrity in the neural network, but it looks to me a lot like a strategy of self-preservation. It's hard to regard this selective forgetting as an engineering flaw when the perfectly designed and incorruptible system is the one that can deliver a lethal jolt.

3. Climacterics

"Man, I want to die, is all," cried Ploy.

"Don't you know," said Dahoud, "that life

is the most precious possession you have?"

"Ho, ho," said Ploy through his tears. "Why?"

"Because," said Dahoud, "without it you'd be dead."

—**Thomas Pynchon,** *V.*

My wife is, among many other things, a teacher, and like all true teachers a student as well, with a serious and scholarly interest in the idea of cycle and recurrence, whether manifest in the repetitions of history, the designs of nature, or the patterns that unfold in people simply because they are alive. Heeding these matters has made her, among many other things, wise in the ways of the human heart, and she has long maintained a theory, based on empirical observation, that at regular intervals of about ten years, we are compelled—whether we like or not, and for the most part we don't—to renegotiate our lives. This is a good deal different from merely undergoing change.

The theory is not without precedent and falls into an intellectual tradition that extends through classical antiquity, back at least to the Old Testament, and quite probably further than that. In its basic form, the idea holds that the life of a human being progresses through specific and well-defined stages. The Greek philosophers, with their passion for order and love of mathematics, imposed a formal, numerical scheme on the whole affair, based on the numbers seven and ten, to which, for various reasons, the highest juju attached. The life of a man was divided into seven-year periods called "hebdomads," and each represented a distinct phase of existence—infant, little child, child, lad, young man, and so on. At each seven-year turning point you became, in a sense, a different person with different attributes, prospects, and responsibilities. Each stage was unique, though certain ages carried with them a particular significance; age forty-nine, for instance, the magic seven times itself, "produces," says Macrobius in his *Commentary on the Dream of Scipio*, "the age which is properly considered and called perfect, so that a man of this age, as one who has already attained and not yet passed perfection, is considered ripe in wisdom and not unfit for the exercise of his physical powers." Seventy years, that is, ten hebdomads, was considered the full span of human life—the same, in fact, as the biblical allotment of three score and ten. Although the specific numbers sometimes got tinkered with along the way, this scheme endured into the nineteenth century, perhaps because the notion was tidily formulated and made a rough kind of sense.

I find my wife's version, however, an improvement, more consistent with experience, and certainly better suited to an age that was brought up waiting for Godot. It posits no providential scheme, no sense of progress, no regular transitions leading to wisdom as the final stage. The only inevitability is the regular occurrence of the critical junctures themselves. Ten years, of course, is just an approximation; the renegotiation might be precipitated sooner by a crisis or by a change of fortune or delayed by a long stretch living on automatic pilot. But even in the absence of these things, sooner or later, unavoidably and inescapably, you come face to face with the fact that things are now different. Something has shrunk and no longer fits, and whether it is you or the world you exist in is the consuming question, though in the end an irrelevant one. Because only three things are certain. First, it is never pretty, this feeling that you have somehow become separated from your own life, that it has disappeared down a shithole somewhere and left you to carry on alone. Second, the attempts to retrieve it are just as unpleasant and bear a disheartening resemblance to a man trying to assemble a large jigsaw puzzle while skydiving. And third, the world is not a flexible place; you are the most adjustable part of the equation, the only real candidate for the necessary alterations. Every decade or so you wake up to the fact that your brain has ended up making a lot of choices that you never really noticed, and you've become a somewhat different person, in different circumstances, with different thoughts and perspectives, all housed in a different body, the latest in a set of increasingly inferior mortal coils. So you begin the labor of examining how all these things might fit together and maybe in the process add a little more to the accumulating understanding that life is essentially tragic, which is altogether separate from the question of whether or not you are happy.

But the important part is this: if you do the thing honestly and begin at the beginning, the first point to address in renegotiating your life is whether you wish it to continue. The answer may be easy or difficult, but only after it is settled can you sit down and begin to talk terms.

4. Nomination

Name, though it seem but a superficial and outward matter,

yet it carrieth much impression and enchantment.

—Francis Bacon

Bacon is right, and it is a most peculiar thing, this power in a name. You may spend a great deal of time outdoors, say on a spring creek, and one day, for whatever reason, a certain species of plant catches your attention. Because you have seen it once, you recognize it again whenever you run across it, and little by little, over the course of a few seasons, you take note of its particulars—that the purple-and-yellow bloom is, except for the color, quite like that of a pepper plant, and in fact so are the leaves; that it prefers the shade, sometimes growing as a freestanding plant but more often vining up or over other vegetation; that it doesn't mind, as gardeners say, having its feet wet and often roots at the very edge of the stream; that a single plant may contain flowers, unripe green berries, and ripe ones like tiny plum tomatoes, all simultaneously; that you have never seen bees visit the blooms, though something must pollinate it. The plant itself and the sight of it become entirely familiar, and you know where it first appears in the spring, and when it dies back in the fall, and what it looks like when the leaves are brown and desiccated but the vine still hangs on to pendulous clusters of miniature red fruit.

Then one day you learn, from a field guide or from someone else, that it is called "bittersweet nightshade." And nothing is quite the same after that. You feel as though you now know the plant in some way that you did not before, that it is in some indefinable sense more familiar to you, though your understanding of the actual plant has not grown or changed in the least. The only difference is that you now know its name.

It is possible, of course, that the name might bear some relation to the object in question—like "stinging nettle" or "hummingbird"—that tells you something about it, though chances are it's something you've already figured out on your own. But the name could just as well be deceiving or inaccurate, conferred out of misapprehension or superstition. The nighthawk, for instance, a bird often seen wheeling on falconlike wings above a trout stream, was once called a "goatsucker" out of the mistaken belief that it engaged in this difficult-to-visualize behavior; and even "nighthawk" is not much closer, since the bird is neither nocturnal nor a raptor. It's also likely that the name is for all practical purposes meaningless, like "daffodil" or "sparrow," which don't seem to have any particular relation at all to their objects, though they once did to someone, somewhere. And though within every name is an archaeology of stories, they are usually stories we have not excavated, and the power of the name is not dependent on knowing them. It is not the particular name but the fact of a name that matters.

The knowledge acquired in learning a name runs no further than the name itself, which is an outward and artificial thing—"superficial," as Bacon calls it—but the impression of knowing goes much deeper and is authentic. When a child learning to speak first names its parents, you can see and hear an unmistakable delight that is not merely the satisfaction of knowing something but the child's thrill in knowing that it knows it, a sense of something gained beyond the mere acquisition of a word. In my budding-young-naturalist years as a child, I used to venture out for the day with binoculars and a butterfly net, and look for birds and capture bugs. Then I would religiously submit each specimen to the Procrustean bed of *The Little Golden Book of Birds*, or *The Handbook of Agricultural Pests, 1961*, my only two field guides, until I had successfully tortured an identification out of it. And even though I was wrong in almost every instance, I had that same sense of a new knowledge that exceeded the weight of a few syllables. Even now, I can look at a cluster of stars in the night sky, recognize its shape, and notice how its position shifts with the changing seasons. But if I learn that it is called "Cassiopeia," I can never look at it in quite the same way again, can never see it without summoning the word that identifies it.

The name of a thing stands midway between the thing itself and our idea of it, anchoring one to the other and fixing them both. There is a gap between what is us and what is not, and names are, literally, the terms with which we negotiate the distance. They invest the world with a familiarity and order that are specifically human, for the birds and plants and stars do not name themselves or one another, nor need the names we give them. But for us, names are a way that the mind and even the heart make an elemental kind of contact with the world and come to establish a form of intimacy with it. It is telling, I think, that when we use the word "anonymous" we draw no real distinction between the colloquial sense of "unknown" and the more etymologically precise one of "without a name." To be without names is to be adrift in an anonymous world.

We are, for better or worse, creatures of words, and names connect to a part of ourselves that can be accessed in no other way. To learn them is a primary act that forges a fundamental and intimate connection. Names stake a claim, an appropriation without ownership, a point of contact with what lies outside of ourselves, with the rest of nature, and with the community that shares our words. Names are a bargain struck with the fact the we are compelled to engage the world through story. They are both a compass with which we locate ourselves and a kind of map we make of the territory. A part of being alive is the search for words that articulate and explain experience, which is not to say that the one with the largest lexicon wins. No one ever really wins. But the names of things are how we bear the world in mind.

10

Beating the Bounds

≈≈≈≈≈≈≈≈

stay together

learn the flowers

go light

—Gary Snyder, "For the Children"

There was for centuries a custom widespread among the towns, villages, and parishes of England, and while written records of it date back to the late medieval period, there can be little doubt that the tradition was already firmly established by then. It took place forty days after Easter, during the three days prior to Ascension Day known as the Rogation Days. Although this annual observance was officially slated on the religious calendar, everything about it had the sniff of one of those older pre-Christian rituals that were grafted onto the ecclesiastical vine so that the church could reap its quota of souls. On the appointed day, the townspeople—farmers and tradesmen, their wives and children, and whatever dignitaries the place had to offer—gathered together under the superintendence of the local clergyman. Since the average workingman and his family had the day off and fine spring weather was a distinct possibility, it is not hard to imagine that the turnout was good and that high spirits prevailed among the assembly. No doubt the town dogs were drawn out to investigate this curious state of affairs and added to the general liveliness. When all were ready, the rector and town officials, followed by everyone else, began to walk the outermost boundaries of the village or parish as had been determined by grants and deeds, custom, usage, and time out of memory. Since most of the towns were agricultural, a patchwork of fields and pastures, the outlying borders were apt to be irregular in shape, and walking the perimeter of even a small village could take all day.

At certain points along the route, the group stopped, and the clergyman delivered a prayer, asking for pretty much what you'd expect—good weather, good crops, good fortune, and general prosperity for his flock. But the more interesting, and I suspect more efficacious parts of this perambulation occurred at other spots, where the village boundary was designated by some manmade or natural feature—a large tree or rock, a stone marker, a ditch or lake or hedgerow. At such points, the participants struck the tree or marker with a peeled willow stick as a way of publicly acknowledging the border and confirming its communal legitimacy. An even more compelling aim of the ritual, in an age when local maps were rare and much land not yet surveyed, was to acquaint the younger generations with these boundaries. Judging by the way such introductions were handled, it appears as though commanding the undivided attention of a ten-year-old boy on a holiday ramble was as difficult then as it is now. So the members of the procession would impress the significance of these borders more or less literally on the young lads among them—by taking the boys and bumping their heads against a boundary marker (often suspending them by their heels first) or throwing them into a hedge or pond. Or sometimes, dispensing with these intermediate ceremonies, they would apply the willow switch directly to selected heads, shoulders, and backsides. The whole thing sounds a little sadistic, but it was by most accounts a pretty good-humored affair, moments of clerical solemnity punctuating longer intervals of secular merriment and practical jokes that, one would guess, approached rowdiness at times. Although the day set aside for the occasion was designated as one of fasting, there were refreshments nonetheless, and in some locations, the parish itself sprang for cakes and ale. And unless I'm badly off the mark, I imagine that along the way, stories were told and retold at specific places, about property disputes and settlements, the arrival and departure of families, alterations in the land, tragic or comic events that occurred here or there over the years, for stories also establish the borders of a common history.

The boundaries were followed without deviation. Should the village holdings extend to a river, a young man chosen as a representative of the processioners would swim it, symbolically reestablishing its authority. By custom, and in some places by law, the congregation was permitted to walk the bounds unhindered. Should some unfortunate have erected a fence or pig shed or even a house that stood in the way, the crowd marched right through it—or worse. One borough, incorporated by Queen Elizabeth, had a specific provision written into its charter; the inhabitants, in their annual circumnavigation, had the right "if it shall seem expedient to them, to cast down, destroy, break, burn all such hedges, walls, ditches, boundaries, houses, house walls, crosses and all other enclosures whatsoever in such a perambulation and to cross back and fro by right freely without let or hindrance by us our heirs or successors and to permit everyone to do so without any payment as they have been in the past. And this as often as it shall please them or seem necessary to them." The axe, mattock, and torch, if not standard equipment, were not altogether strangers to these affairs either. This kind of liberty with other people's property may seem excessive, but the matter of boundaries was, beneath the pranks and celebration, a serious one—a reaffirmation for some participants, a practical education for others. Knowing one's local precincts is always a matter of some weight, and the young, in particular, had to be instilled with a sense of territorial limits: of lines that divide the inside from the out, the trustworthy spaces from the questionable ones; of where and what the jurisdiction of home actually was. So every year the children were, in a manner we might presume was unforgettable, shown precisely those things.

This custom, depending upon where and when it was practiced, was called "processioning," "perambulating the parish," "rogationing," "riding the fringes," and "common riding," among other things, but the name that has survived and is most often used now is "beating the bounds." And though the bounds were not all that was beaten, I believe even the English would have regarded "beating the boys" as an unfortunate choice of terms for a practice designed in part to solicit God's mercy and goodwill. I find no small charm in this name, "beating the bounds," even aside from its inadvertent reference to a certain national zeal in administering the switch, ferule, or pandy bat at the first whiff of opportunity. "Beating" suggests the rhythmic regularity and constancy that are at the center of all rituals, and from the same etymological root grows another branch of the word "beat" that is still used today by cops, salesmen, and anglers to specify a prescribed home territory for their respective employments.

This tradition continued for better than half a millennium, its particulars shifting some in the changing winds of politics and religion, before finally petering out in the nineteenth century, although its cultural importance probably waned a good deal before the institution itself dwindled away. I understand that in some places in England the custom is now being revived, but in my experience, historical resuscitations of this kind always have a self-conscious and unconvincing quality about them, like people desperately trying to look at ease in rented formalwear. But the conditions of modern life, I think, do not favor recovering the original and complex significance of the ritual—part religious, part civil, part tribal.

And part animal. For beating the bounds is nothing if not animal behavior. A great many creatures, from chickadees to house cats to grizzly bears, patrol the borders of their territory, announce them to the sight or scent or hearing of others, and in general keep track of their turf. We share this instinct in some form, though we no longer have need of its original animal purpose since we define and protect our territories in other ways now. But the impulse persists. I live, for example, near the center of a smallish town in a neighborhood of smallish lots, and what little yard space exists is often given over to flower and vegetable gardens, the whole of which might be taken in at a single glance from the kitchen window. Yet it is not uncommon, on a summer's evening, to find people strolling through their yards, examining the spring plantings, pulling a weed here or there, pointing to the peeling paint on a garage, or scuffing a toe at a crack in the sidewalk heaved up by the root of a linden tree. They may be mentally making notes on what needs doing, or checking in on things, or just enjoying the evening, but if you watch them, they will in time walk a circuit of their small property. It is not a conscious gesture of territoriality, but they are beating the bounds nonetheless.

And those bounds need not be large, or even outdoors. I engage in a habit that I used to think was a little peculiar but have since discovered is not all that uncommon. When I return home from an extended trip, get my luggage inside, and click on the thermostat or open the windows, depending on the season, I begin wandering about the house in a fashion that might fairly be called aimless. It's more instinct than intention, not something I set out to do but that I catch myself doing, moving from room to room, making the rounds over and over, the number of cycles proportional to the length of my absence. I suppose I might, in some vague sense, be "making sure everything's okay," though this attributes a consciousness of purpose that it doesn't actually possess, and in any case I'm too travel-stunned as a rule to execute even that kind of low-order function. I'm not looking for anything in particular, for signs of intrusion, for something missing or disturbed, can't say, in fact, that I'm really looking at all, just . . . behaving. If I set myself to something useful, pouring a glass of beer and sorting through a mountain of mail, before long and without realizing it, I'm back up again, glass in hand, ambling through the house on a strange kind of auto-pilot. Then there comes a point, maybe after fifteen minutes, maybe in a couple of hours, when all of a sudden, at some level and in some unspecified way, I appear to be satisfied, and the whole episode comes to an end. Other people have told me that they do much the same thing.

I can't explain what drives this impulse; it is so motive-less and involuntary that it must be wedged deep in some animal part of the brain. But the outcome, I think, is recognizably human, if only because it is somewhat paradoxical.

To beat these interior bounds is, in a literal sense, to make one's self at home, to become reacquainted with intimate locality, even though its every detail is already familiar. But who's to say?—maybe grizzly bears feel just the same way. It's no surprise that in this semiconscious meandering about, the room to which I return most often and in which I remain the longest is my study, the place most surely outfitted with the accouterments of myself, a minor calamity of fly rods and tying gear and tackle, desks and shelves and books. Simply registering a physical presence there orients me again to the life and the person who lived it that were left behind when I packed my bags; it replots the coordinates of that peculiar sense of identity that is allied with space.

Getting one's bearings in the world like this is an intermittent but ongoing project, more difficult at some times than others. And when that world becomes a diminished place, it becomes necessary to locate its boundaries once again, map out the new territory, and find its terms. Like any survey, it requires a starting point, some square one, no matter how arbitrary it may be in the beginning or prove in the end.

For a few seasons, in our mid-twenties, my brother and I beat the bounds along a certain section near the middle of Jerusalem Creek. It was nothing that we planned or one day deliberately decided to undertake, just a whim at first. That we found ourselves on this particular piece of water, however, was not altogether accidental. The upstream end was marked by a pool, the widest and deepest on the stream. Because of its size, this pool was both the easiest spot to fish on all of Jerusalem Creek and the one, we assumed, that held the largest trout; the contradiction lurking in these two simultaneous notions never once occurred to us. But from our earliest trips to driftless country, it was the place we almost always began a day's fishing. Already a familiar starting point in one respect, then, it was only natural, I suppose, that it become the starting point for our beating of the bounds. The tail of the pool tapered to a shallow sluice you could almost jump across and then funneled the water into a corridor of hardwoods, mostly oaks. This narrow band of trees extended only a short distance outward from either bank of the creek, a ribbon of vegetation left standing when the adjacent land was cleared who knows how long ago. A screen of undergrowth rose up beneath the spreading limbs, and when you worked the water within, you had the convincing impression of fishing in a forest even though the wooded area was in fact quite small. Here and there, the stream veered beyond the trees for a moment, cutting a bend in the meadow before returning. Farther downstream, the trees thinned out but grew much larger, a broad canopy still shading the water. And beyond that, the trees disappeared altogether, and the creek flowed through a short plot of open meadow that contained what I once regarded as the sweetest fifty feet of trout stream on earth, a little run where I caught a brook, brown, and rainbow trout, all wild, all in one morning. From there, the creek ran beneath a little bridge on a little-used two-lane blacktop. This entire stretch of water wandered through a long, thin right triangle of land—the base marked by the big pool, the perpendicular leg by a line of hills on the western edge of the valley, the hypotenuse by the road. Creek, hills, and highway all converged at a sharp point on the downstream end. The triangle enclosed no more than twenty acres of land, probably less, but because of its narrow shape and the meandering of the channel, it contained perhaps half a mile of water. Throughout most of its length, the stream hugged the toe of the ridge on the west, leaving an open expanse to the east that had been put in pasture, grazed in some summers and not in others, but easy walking either way.

This stretch was not the best fishing water on Jerusalem Creek (a certain fifty feet excepted) and was, I think, nearer the worst, though by and large the difference between the two was not terribly great; the stream fished pretty consistently throughout. Even so, we always thought that this section—under all that shade and tucked against the hills that put it in shadow well before evening—should have been better than the rest. True, the channel tended more to a gentle sway than exaggerated curling and so might have been a trifle short on those hairpin bends that produce the deepest and most promising corners. But it had its share of good spots and its share of trout. That it seemed to us there should have been more perhaps testifies only to the ordinary fact that, like most fishermen, we gauged the excellence of the water by the number of fish we took, which is a poor yardstick to begin with and particularly so when wielded by poor fishermen. Looking back now, I suspect that this water was well supplied with trout of the usual two varieties: the kind we could catch, which were scarce, and the kind we could not, which were abundant. But we couldn't complain, and didn't. From end to end, it offered a solid morning's fishing in a greater variety of surroundings than you normally find on a spring creek, and in a purely visual sense was quite a handsome reach of water.

This became our beat, and for a few summers we returned to it faithfully on each trip to driftless country, though I couldn't say just how it happened that we took to walking its bounds. The precedent may have been set by a habit that Gecko and I developed not long after we began fly fishing and have continued ever since. At some point during a day on the water, sometimes by arrangement, sometimes spontaneously, we meet up and share a rod, switching off on each trout risen, or maybe each one caught, or just alternating good-looking spots when the fishing is slow. This is not an efficient way to cover water—appalling to the body counters, I'm sure—but I still find it among the most satisfying. For one thing, like many fly fisherman, I enjoy watching another angler fish nearly as much as I enjoy fishing myself, and on some occasions even more. It is the most contemplative version of something I find contemplative to begin with, and its rewards lie in the observation rather than the action. Watching somebody fish is a good deal more like watching baseball, a slow-paced game with studied aspects, than it is like watching, say, a stock-car race, where spectators gather in the simple-hearted hope of witnessing catastrophe. To split a rod with someone is a leisurely thing, and if that someone is any good, watching him lay out a cast and drop the fly and work the water feels very much like fishing, even though you're not holding the rod. The stakes are low because you are there in part for the companionship, and if you choose your partner wisely, the company is always good no matter what the fishing is like. Still, the specifics vary; some days the two of us stand elbow to elbow, knee-deep in the current, both concentrating on a rising fish or a choice piece of water, studying the work at hand, and whatever we have to say is confined to shop talk. Other times, one of us sits on the bank while the other casts lazily, and the conversation turns to other things. Whatever happens, the arrangement has proven agreeable enough that we haven't altered the pattern in thirty years. Even Lizard, who is by nature more workmanlike on the water, has come to enjoy it of late, now that the brutish life of a junior faculty member has kicked a little of the starch out of him.

Our beating of the bounds, I imagine, grew from this practice of sharing a rod, though you can't fish, alone or in company, and beat the bounds at the same time. They are related but finally separate enterprises, each of which requires too much attention to admit the other. So unlike the English villagers, we carried no rod, willow or otherwise, nor was one necessary to our purposes. Our circuit of the water always began at the big pool, and so we ended up walking downstream, not the angler's preferred direction but not without its charm either, and usually on the pasture side, which presented little in the way of undergrowth or obstacles. We walked the bank slowly, stopping to examine whatever caught the eye—an unusual plant or wildflower, bird, insect, or any of the small curiosities in which the natural world abounds. At one time, the meadows were host to a great many monarch butterflies, though their numbers have dwindled since then, and we spent some time looking over the milkweed plants for the fat, flamboyantly banded caterpillars. Sometimes we would find a monarch chrysalis, an elegantly formed and polished structure of translucent jade, trimmed in a circle of tiny obsidian dots and metallic gold flecks, a thing that looks more mineral than animal. We once discovered, hidden in a kinnikinnick bush, a hummingbird's nest—the only one I have ever seen—woven of the finest threads of plant fiber and spiderweb, perfect and precisely shaped, like a child's teacup, containing two pearly little eggs. In late summer, the tall grass was filled with the webs of *Argiope* spiders, creatures of a velvety jet black streaked in sunflower yellow, with bodies the size of acorns. The webs were large, elaborate arrays of concentric polygons, some two feet in diameter; each web converged on a center crosshatched with zigzags of white silk so suggestive of cursive script that some people call these orb spinners "writing spiders." After a humid night, the silk was strung with droplets of dew that sparked in the sunlight. Like anglers everywhere, we paid closest attention to the webs near the bank for clues to the previous evening's hatch—most often the rusty spinners of blue-wing olive duns, or small caddis, or sometimes a medium-sized mayfly (never identified) that I'd come across only once or twice while fishing. But these were incidental catches; grasshoppers were the mainstay, and in the fall, the fields adjacent to the stream were alive with them.

As we went along, though, we mostly studied the water. We weren't looking specifically for trout, but after a time fly fishing recalibrates one's internal radar to zero in on rising fish until it becomes impossible to pass by water, even the most turbid and scurvy ditch, without some part of the brain scanning for rings. From time to time a trout would rise, the most heartening sight of all on a trout stream and, like a stone marker struck by a willow wand, a small certification that all is as it should be. When we spoke at all, the conversation turned on the stream itself, and we pointed out to each other spots along the way where fish had been caught or lost in the past, or enticing places with dark water where we had never hooked a thing and so drew the angler's predictable conclusion that it was home to some beast, too wise to be hooked, that drove out all the smaller fish. We recounted good and bad days, retelling stories familiar to us both occasioned by places along the way, and it was only natural that we should give them names: First Pool, the Oaks, Pat's Pool, Meadow Bends—a little short on imagination, I concede, but they were intended only as a practical convenience. Yet as names inevitably do, they established a kind of closeness and became another one of the ways in which we knew the place. Even the name I've chose for the stream, Jerusalem Creek, had its origin about this time, a random association with no biblical significance. Rather, we were driving along the creek one afternoon when I first heard a Norman Blake version of the Bill Monroe tune "Jerusalem Ridge," and from that point on I always thought of the steep hills on the western edge of the valley by this name, which I then borrowed for the water.

As a physical system, a spring creek is probably the most stable version of moving water, but in other, smaller ways, it is perhaps the most mutable. A spring creek in late May and that same creek in early September are two quite different places. Each time we beat the bounds, we took note of the accumulating changes of the season—the progress of the aquatic vegetation, the promising little chutes formed by new growths of weed, the shady and protected spots made as bankside grasses drooped over the stream under the burden of ripening seed heads. We discussed the fishing possibilities they presented and marked them for later. The changes from year to year were subtler—a bend pool that nibbled its way a little farther into the meadow, a riffly glide that was deepening or filling in by degrees. Small islands sometimes formed over the course of a few seasons. A mound of water weed would establish itself midstream, trapping waterborne silts that settled to the bottom in a mound and became a rooting medium for new shoots. These in turn filtered even more sediments, piling them higher and higher until they touched the surface and were at last colonized by water-loving terrestrial plants. The new island altered the flow of currents, shunting them aside at new angles and changing the shape of the fishing for some distance downstream. Or such an island might succumb to slow erosion, the current winning this round, but again remaking the stream below it into a new arrangement of runs and seams and eddies. Detecting these slower, less conspicuous changes required a close familiarity with the place, and we took, if not pride, a certain satisfaction in knowing the water well enough to recognize the small increments of difference from one summer to the next.

We sat for a while at the places a fisherman would naturally choose, a high, grassy bank with a good view of the stream up and down or the narrow tongue of an oxbow almost surrounded by water. Near the bottom of our beat, a great oak limb had broken away from the trunk. The tree was not lightning scorched, and a mature oak does not surrender its branches without a fight, even in a high wind; it must have died of insects or disease and then split off of its own weight. It had fallen in a level pasture right at the edge of an open piece of water where it caught the afternoon shade; it was barkless and smooth and perfect for sitting. From there, a few minutes' walk brought us to the little bridge that marked the downstream limit of our water. We climbed a low embankment and walked the county road back to where we'd parked, near the big pool.

≈≈≈≈≈≈≈≈≈

And that, I must admit, is about all there really was—no moments of high drama, no beseeching the divine for a personal favor, no eventful culmination, little enough to distinguish it from an ordinary walk in the country, except perhaps that kind of temporary solace that comes with familiar return. And this is not inconsiderable, worthy enough at least to be the subject of many very old myths. Beating the bounds became one of those small rituals in life by which we locate ourselves for a while, that answer to the part of us that finds a foothold in a thing known for certain. There is comfort in traveling a well-known territory, a balm in its intimate details, an assurance that all that's beautiful does not drift away like the waters. We never beat the bounds in the vain hope of finding it all unchanged, just as before; the changes were often the most interesting part, but always on a scale and at a pace that could be accommodated. It had about it the feel of looking through an album of photographs you already know well, picking out the faces and noting how each is different now but, despite the changes, still recognizable and reassuringly itself. And the most enduring sense in the end was one of continuity that came to encompass not only the place and occasion of our ritual but the act itself. There are moments and places tucked invisibly into the background of a life that can at times extend outward and make themselves felt out of proportion to their size, can give, if only for a while, order and perspective to the larger outline of things, like the vanishing point in a drawing.

Rituals, even those of loss, are by nature an affirmation, and their significance is cumulative. In ours, meaning grew along a trout stream; the landscape gave rise to ritual that in turn conferred a kind of sanctity on the land. And this is what it means, I think, to know a place by heart.

11

Green Thoughts in
a Green Shade

~~~~~~~

Meanwhile the mind, from pleasure less,

Withdraws into its happiness;

The mind, that ocean where each kind

Does straight its own resemblance find;

Yet it creates, transcending these,

Far other worlds and other seas;

Annihilating all that's made

To a green thought in a green shade.

—Andrew Marvell, "The Garden"

"I hear what you are talking about," said the wife. "But you will make no impression on Humphrey. As long as the fish rise to his bait, everybody is what he ought to be. Bless you, Casaubon has got a trout stream, and does not care about fishing it himself: could there be a better fellow?"

193

"Well, there is something in that," said the Rector, with his

quiet, inward laugh. "It is a very good quality in a man

to have a trout stream."

—George Eliot, *Middlemarch*

Prior to settlement, the driftless area marked a zone of transition between the hardwood forests of the East and the mesic, tallgrass prairie to the west. Two centuries of human habitation have altered both of these great natural ecosystems almost beyond recognition, but spring-creek country still preserves something of its original borderland character, with open ridge tops and plateaus between hill slopes covered in a mixed forest that encroaches on the valleys from the edges and sneaks in along the banks of streams. Although I have lived now for almost twenty years in the Pacific Northwest, wandering and fishing among its vast tracts of Douglas fir and Ponderosa pine, I remain a victim of my own provincialism and still much prefer these eastern woods. The coniferous forests are beautiful places; symmetrical, almost formal, geometries of cones and spires, they draw the eye upward in a landscape that is overwhelmingly vertical, majestic, and humbling. But I find such places, splendid as they are, a little uniform, monochromatic, and unapproachable when compared to a hardwood forest. The forms in a deciduous woods are rounded and fan-shaped, spreading into a ceiling that invites the eye to a horizontal axis and creates the sense not of dramatic and rising space but of a local and interior one. It is a more complex place in a visual sense because it is more varied in a biological one, each species of tree contributing a distinct signature that can be read in the shape of its silhouette against the sky, the color and detail of a leaf, the texture of bark, the spacing and full-ness of limbs. But on a hot day in a humid midwestern sum-mer, you come to appreciate that the many and various architectural details of a single tree are best expressed simul-taneously in the type of shade that it casts.

The broad leaves of a big sugar maple throw a solid and serviceable shade, heavy enough to stay cool and unbroken even in windy weather. Elm is good for shading a house; its smaller, paler, sparser leaves produce a lighter shade of shade that gives relief from the sun but lets in plenty of light through the windows. Fruit trees are more variable. Pruned for bearing, they are almost worthless for shade, but left un-tended—like the ancient Gravenstein in my backyard—they may divide into multiple trunks with a broad canopy that is comfortable and open beneath. For a dark, heavy-duty shade, I would choose a big chestnut with the rounded, swelling shape of a cumulus cloud, though these have been all but eradicated by blight and the large ones exist now only as cul-tivated specimens. The shade of a large black walnut is per-haps the most beautiful of all for watching. The elliptical, saw-toothed leaves grow in a fernlike array and produce a delicate fretwork of shadows on the ground, a filigree of soft green that sifts the light like freshly milled flour. Even in a mild breeze, this dappling shifts and flickers like sunlight on a trout stream. One of the spring creeks we fished from time to time, Mariposa Creek, had a beautiful grove of walnuts growing along the bank, and it is difficult to imagine a more soothing place to sit and watch the play of light and shadow on a bright afternoon.

But for a fine, all-purpose, workmanlike shade, nothing surpasses that of a mature white oak, heavy-limbed and spreading, its lowermost branches head-high, its glossy leaves casting a deep and deep-green shade. It was under just such a shade, on a warm midsummer day, sitting on an oak limb fallen by the water, in the course of beating the bounds along Jerusalem Creek, that Gecko and I first began speculating about a matter that every serious fisherman eventually comes round to: "What would it be like to own a trout stream?" Not a whole trout stream of course, or anything large or famous, just a small piece of unpresuming water with decent fishing, identical in fact to the very water we were studying at the moment.

This question, I think, is more or less inevitable, a natural stage in the curious, ongoing relationship that a fisherman forges with moving water. It takes time to know a trout stream, but if you visit one often enough to learn at least some of its secrets and idiosyncrasies, you begin to fish the water not only with a greater expectation of success but with an increasing sense of affectionate familiarity, even on those days when the trout hand you your hat. After a time, this fondness gives way to a feeling of proprietorship about the place, which at its best shows itself in a paternal kind of protectiveness. But like most things human, it is rarely at its best and more typically takes the form of indignant glances and territorial posturing when one angler discovers another fishing "his" water, not water that belongs to him but to which he feels entitled by long association. Direct confrontations seldom result (unless a certain species of fishing guide happens to be involved); it can lead, however, to a lot of under-the-breath muttering, resentment, impatience, and the kind of vibes that make unpleasant company on a trout stream.

This is not an angler's finest hour. If you fish the water long enough you may pass out of this phase, into something that might be called a sense of stewardship—not a feeling that the place is yours but only that it is your responsibility, and in a way that has less to do with the conduct of other people than with the way you yourself behave. It is the frame of mind most conducive to appreciating a trout stream even when you aren't fishing it. The step from passion to possession, however, is generally a short one, and the idea of volunteer stewardship at some point suggests the thought of a legal one. Though we may not follow out this suggestion very far, it is a rare angler who does not, if only on some abstract level, entertain the thought of just how fine it would be to have a little bit of the place all to himself. Fishing is essentially a utopian occupation, and this is its natural extension.

My brother and I were hardly exceptions, and in our case the process was aided by the well-formulated bounds we beat, framed by distinct natural and man-made features, a self-contained parcel of a size modest enough to permit the thought of ownership. We did not arrive at the notion of acquiring a piece of trout water all at once; it evolved by degrees from humbler beginnings. We camped out a fair amount in those days, and finding a spot to pitch a tent in farm country was no simple task; finding a spot on the banks of a stream—an absolute prerequisite in our eyes—was almost impossible. We did have our customary place on the upper part of Jerusalem Creek, but for various reasons it had never been altogether satisfactory and grew less so every season. Locating a new spot became an enduring objective of our scouting trips, but except for one or two questionable possibilities, we never found a suitable place to set up a tent, spread around some chairs, pile out our stuff, and indulge in the kind of tenement-camping for which we already showed a startling aptitude.

Sitting under the oak shade one afternoon and watching the water go by, Gecko pointed out, just in passing, that a certain plot of ground just downstream of the big pool on the opposite side of the creek would make an ideal site to pitch camp. I could not disagree; it was level enough, private, and shaded for much of the day. Talking over its various virtues, it occurred to us that while we had walked the bounds of this triangular piece of territory regularly for a couple of seasons, we had no idea who owned it. His cows appeared in the pasture from time to time, but never the man himself. We never once saw him fishing, or beating the bounds, or just sitting on a fallen oak limb breathing in his great good fortune at having such a place. It wasn't even clear where he might live. The nearest working farm was a mile away, but that meant nothing. In a terrain where most of the useful agricultural land was fragmented into small plots, it wasn't unusual for a farmer to hold or lease a number of scattered territories. Still, there were records and deeds that could be consulted, and we wondered if he might give us permission to camp there, maybe for "a small annual fee," as we vaguely described it to ourselves. Maybe he was a decent sort, and all it would take was asking. Fishermen, the naïve and desperate in particular, will sometimes delude themselves with this kind of hopeful fantasy, even as they know deep down there isn't a prayer.

Setting aside that question for a moment, we turned our minds to the place itself, admitting that while it was already a first-rate spot, a little bit of work could transform it from the merely excellent to the absolutely perfect. It did not, for instance, have potable water, though in a country so rich in aquifers, drilling a low-volume well would be neither difficult nor expensive. When we considered, with some misgiving, the Disneyesque scale of our tent, a wooden platform seemed a good idea—a more consistent foundation, off the ground, more comfortable. How hard could it be to build one? And if a person was going to that effort, it would make sense to extend the front of the platform four or five feet outward for a kind of sitting porch, with a rail to put your feet on. Gecko suggested a roof for shade in the midday sun, and I a screen for mosquitoes. While not strictly necessary, an outhouse would be a pleasant convenience—nothing elaborate, maybe just a three-side job open to a view of the ridge on the west. If a truck was already coming to deliver the platform lumber, might as well do it all at once.

These and the other details we tinkered with showed themselves in a somewhat different light, however, when illuminated by the dawning recognition that no landowner was likely to tolerate such embellishments, even for a small annual fee. I recall that it was Gecko who first broached the subject, wondering aloud if this unknown person might be persuaded to sell the land and, if so, what the price might be. I was surprised because I had never known (nor would I ever meet) a person more suspicious about acquiring possessions, mistrustful of the motives and mechanisms and consequences of owning things. On the other hand, he had just finished graduate school a month or two earlier, was on the brink of gainful employment, and had always thought in bigger terms than I did anyway. And besides, this was a trout stream, which automatically exempted it from ordinary categories; exceptional places, perhaps, demanded extraordinary measures. At the time, an acre of prime midwestern farmland sold for slightly less than I earned annually in the indentured servitude of graduate teaching. But fertile as it was, the property in question was not prime land—small, a little isolated, cut into irregular pieces by the stream that ran through it. We went back and forth about what it might be worth but lacked the particulars to make any headway on the matter. A little legwork could have settled the issue for certain, but we had come nowhere near exhausting the pleasure of thinking about it, and so instead of meeting it head-on, we resorted to a kind of rhetorical flanking maneuver. Two cases, we agreed, were possible: the land was for sale, or it wasn't. We thought it reasonable enough to assume, simply for the sake of argument, that a deal could be worked out, and its specifics posed a separate problem that would need to be addressed separately.

I am perhaps misrepresenting somewhat the course of our speculations. The ideas we entertained did not burst forth full-blown in a single, enthusiastic afternoon; they took shape a bit at a time, during many walks along our beat on Jerusalem Creek. We talked over each detail, discussed its merits and flaws, and made modifications as they appeared necessary. We mentally cordoned off those areas that required more information or deliberation—the details of well drilling and outhouse construction, for instance—and filed them away for the future, since the trick in this sort of thing is to keep an eye on the big picture without becoming derailed by technicalities. At the same time, we believed ourselves reasonable and cautious people, not given to impulsive whim, not easily unmoored from planet Earth and swept up to castles in the clouds. We held the idea of buying a trout stream at arm's length, consciously distancing ourselves from the alluring penumbra of pure fantasy that radiated from its core. Our talk, at once specific and hypothetical, was the talk of people trying on a thought for size, going into detail but still maintaining a prudent detachment, never saying, for instance, "Once we build the platform, we can . . ." but rather, "A guy that owned this place might think about digging a well . . ." More than a daydream but less than a plan, the ideas we envisioned fell into that indefinite imaginative space of the plausible that lies halfway between the two.

Only once did we really get a bit carried away, but the specific temptation struck a chord so harmonious with our own impulses that for a time we composed a little melody to accompany it. We stumbled upon a spring creek while scouting one day. I don't recall whether or not it was a certified "Wisconsin trout stream"—it never yielded a single fish— but we returned time and again for a different reason. Typical in most respects, the stream had one unique feature: an old mill beside a small milldam, and along the tailrace below, a splendidly bucolic little spot with a cool, grassy bank shaded in tall trees and awash in the calming rhythms of the turning mill wheel and the sound of falling water. If the mill and pond did not date to the original settlement of the place, they went back very nearly that far. The mill itself had been carefully and lovingly restored to its original operating condition, and the dam well-maintained for that purpose; it was a perfectly picturesque spot, and we often timed our travels to have lunch there. What intrigued us though, apart from the quiet congeniality of the place, was a small concrete sluiceway that, at some unknown time in the past, had been built at one end of the dam. An old iron rack-and-screw mechanism raised and lowered a wooden sluice gate that controlled the flow of water through the concrete chute. It was in some disrepair and clearly had not been used for a long time, but on the bank beside it, hidden by the overgrown weeds, were the rusted remains of a small turbine fan that fit at the end of the penstock. I have no idea who installed it, or when, or why it was abandoned, but it must have once generated electrical power for the house nearby, or perhaps an older one that once stood in its place.

This was something that had never occurred to us, and we were instantly taken with the marvelous tidiness, the clean self-containment of the idea, and began considering similar possibilities for our own section of water—a cabin, maybe even a small house, instead of tent platform; a spot at the tail of the big pool that might be suitable for low-head hydro generation. Though these conjectures marked a decided change in direction—from a better camping spot to a different kind of life—the independence and self-sufficiency they represented appealed to us irresistibly. Or perhaps to be more accurate, they appealed to me. The previous two years had been rough going, and I wanted, or believed I wanted, to chuck it all and just hide out for a while away from things, in the way that people sometimes confuse renouncing the world with solving their problems. One of the stories I was fond of repeating at the time concerned Ernest Hemingway's younger brother Leicester. In the mid-1960s, Leicester hammered together an eight-by-thirty-foot floating wooden platform, towed it seven miles off the coast of Jamaica, anchored it there with a Ford engine block, and declared himself a separate country. I wasn't sure of his reasons and so naturally assumed they were identical to mine, and I believed I knew just how he felt. Gecko entertained this quasi-homesteading notion with as much seriousness and objectivity as he did our other ideas, but I think for the most part he was only humoring me in a fraternal sort of way. His own life was headed squarely into the world, not away from it, and he was not in any case prone to the dramatic gesture. And though the idea, with its little dam and turbine, never lost its charm for me, the practical requirements, beginning with the fact that we didn't have a dime between us, became too insistent to ignore. So we set the matter aside to simmer and scaled back our thinking.

We returned our attention to Jerusalem Creek itself. It is a universal fact of trout fishing that no matter how good a stream may be, every angler harbors private notions about how it might be made a little better, how it might conform a bit more closely to that ideal trout stream he carries around in his head. A guy who owned this place, we agreed, could work some interesting improvements on the water, and we began to beat the bounds with this idea in mind. We took each section of the beat in turn and held it up to the light of our imaginations as one might candle an egg, looking for a secret life that might be encouraged to emerge. Of all our speculations, these were the most satisfying. We had no grand designs or wholesale remodeling in mind, just some tinkering and tweaking. The object in this sort of thing is not to dig a new trout stream but to engineer ways in which the current does as much of the heavy lifting as possible. At strategic spots, we imagined small wing deflectors that would shovel the current in one direction to deepen a bend or bank. In our minds, we pinched little throats into the tops of runs to accelerate the current and scour the spawning gravels clean. We turned the flow away from eroding banks to give the vegetation a chance to grow and stabilize the soil. Into a few sandy-bottomed and featureless runs, we rolled limestone rocks to make pockets for the fish and dead water where silt could settle and aquatic weeds take root. Standing deadwood provided the raw material for a couple of miniature dams that would back up the water into pools for rearing the little fish. We worked and reworked our stretch of water, not everywhere, just here and there, trying to envision what would attract the most and biggest trout, give the greatest fishing variety, and best please the eye. And when we had at last roughed out a picture of it all, we asked ourselves the question that must eventually be confronted: would we let anyone else fish it? With no strong opinions either way, we thought it a reasonable compromise to post the water "No Bait, No Kill," to maintain the trout and keep the gunnysackers out. We had no way of knowing that the next few years would see a national trend in the establishment of catch-and-release water and bring with it an instinctive perception on the part of anglers that such places automatically have better fishing. Far from reducing the crowds, posting water with special regulations would prove as effective in discouraging people as a FREE BEER sign at a softball game.

At the time, however, it seemed a mere detail. I had not yet arrived at the deep ambivalence I now hold about private water, and were the whole thing to repeat itself today, the question of access would be the place I'd begin rather than end. The driftless area had plenty of private property, of course, and we'd been shown the door more than once, but I hadn't yet run across those people who felt they owned not only the land but the streambed, the water, all the trout that made a living in it, and the exclusive right to fish them. I have now, and I find it, as a friend of mine says, disturbingly undemocratic, in the small *d* sense of the term.

I get the chance these days, not often and always under somewhat quirky circumstances, to fish private water, both the kind you pay to get on and that rarer and more mysterious kind that no money can buy access to, that you get on only by knowing someone or, as in my case, knowing someone who knows someone. It is an oddly mixed experience. Barring the kind of weather-related calamities that are always possible— too much or too little rain, temperature too hot or too cold— the fishing in these places is, beyond a ghost of a doubt, better than it is on even the best public water on the best trout stream of equivalent character and size—which is what you'd expect, I suppose, but it always surprises me a little anyway. In some cases the number of frighteningly large trout occupying an unbelievably small area of water gives the fishing a kind of artificial, staged quality, like professional wrestling. I was once given permission to fish some exclusive water on the River Test in England (having, I think, been mistaken for someone else) and the number of big trout along a short beat was so unnatural it was almost creepy. And those were just the ones I could see. Apart from catching fish, the fishing experience on private streams has almost always been better as well. The water itself is often gorgeous. People with the means to buy a stretch of river have, almost by definition, enough to afford the best-looking spots. (There have been notable exceptions; some of the ugliest water I've seen has been privately held, but the fishing was still remarkable.) Regardless of the surroundings, you fish in the certainty that you won't see another angler around the next bend or along the next pool. You can work the water at whatever pace you like and indulge the pleasure of a man who has a trout stream entirely to himself. I can never quite manage this without feeling a certain guilt at the same time, a sense that I enjoy an unfair advantage over other anglers, though I think this is what some people like best about it. And even when the fishing is difficult, which it certainly can be, I never quite feel like I've earned whatever success I may have. If all of this sounds a little morally precious, I hasten to add that it has never once prevented me from accepting a single invitation.

Private ownership has saved some trout streams from the damages wrought by ranching, agriculture, development, and if the truth be told, from crowds of fishermen that can hammer a place just by being there, no matter how well-intentioned and careful they may be. "Each man kills the thing he loves," writes Oscar Wilde, and one need look no further than some of the best-known rivers in America to see just how this paradox works. Private water has safeguarded stocks of indigenous fish and protected important spawning habitat, although in a great many cases I think this has been a means to end—money—rather than end in itself. Angling profiteers can crow all they like, and do, about "preserving the resource," but I'm seldom convinced they are talking about anything other than their own bankrolls. Still, there's no dodging the fact that the kind of management made possible by individual ownership has helped some streams, which tempts me to think that it is a good thing, at least on a small scale. But the difficulty arises when the scale is not small, and there are now entire trout rivers in the East and West that are if not technically, then effectively locked up. I find this worrisome.

I've no desire to wage war against private property or incite mobs of outraged fishermen to storm the walls of the privileged class. I can't even say in all honesty that if I had that kind of money I'd behave any differently, and there is added temptation when the claims of the resource and those of self-interest lie in the same direction. Certainly, compromises are possible. Like half the fly fishermen in the country, and most of the ones in the East, Gecko and I once fished the most legendary stretch of the most legendary spring creek on the continent—Charlie Fox's section of the Letort. As we were setting up our rods, the legendary Charlie Fox himself walked down from his house—as indeed I had been told he would—and began talking with us, general pleasantries and fishing chat. (It is strange how you sometimes remember insignificant details; he carried a quart jar of grapefruit juice, sipping from it at intervals, then brushing away the drops that clung to his beard and mustache. And the entire time he spoke, a little black caddis ran back and forth across his thumb.) In the course of our conversation, he told us that after years of fishing and studying this section of the stream, he'd become so attached to the water and the particular trout living there that he could no longer bring himself to fish it. It appeared to me a decision motivated more by aesthetics than ethics, and I admired this form of appreciation that was earth-bound in the particulars of place and at the same time somewhat rarified. Maybe he just faced the fact that few fishermen openly acknowledge—that it is possible to get tired of a piece of water—but I didn't come away with that impression. In either case, it was a strictly personal decision; he didn't prohibit others from fishing his water and in fact seemed to take a keen interest in their doings, gave them advice, wished them well. He just had no desire or need to fish it anymore himself.

I doubt that most anglers could own a piece of water and manage not to fish it, which is fine, but once you admit that even some fishing is acceptable, the rest of it plays out in one of two directions. Either you open up the water, if only in a limited way, and with it open a world of problems, beginning with the health and well-being of the stream, and maybe ending with the kind of complications that other people so often bring, and you'd wonder why you bought the place at all. Or you close it off, cop to a certain selfishness, and own up to the fact that you are just one person keeping a disproportionate share of a highly limited resource all to yourself because, in your construction of the world, you somehow "deserve" it—deserve to enjoy it, or profit from it, or merely to own it— more than anyone else. And this is a deeply unattractive species of vanity. You choose, in short, to be the consummate saint or the supreme asshole, and I don't believe I'm up to either one of these.

Private ownership does sometimes save trout streams, but it also caters to one of the uglier human attributes, which is to grab a little piece of paradise and then pull up the ladder after yourself. And you need only visit certain rivers in Montana to see how that attitude has in the end harmed a great many more places than it has helped. There are not enough Waldens (or for some of us, enough Emersons) for every man to be Thoreau. It may well be a good quality in a person to own a trout stream—depends on the person—but for most of us, it is probably a better quality not to.

It was not, however, out of some virtuousness that we never bought that stretch of water along Jerusalem Creek, or looked into buying it, or even inquired about camping on it. Nor did our visions collapse of their own weight or evaporate out of sheer insubstantiality. They just receded into the background, little by little, as we began fishing other, better, spring creeks more and more often, and beat the bounds of our small stretch of water less and less, until finally not at all, though I couldn't say exactly when it ended. I've looked back on those events many times since, but never once with the feeling of mothballed aspirations or regret for the road not taken, for I think I see them now in a truer light, in the awareness of the thousand compromises that living entails. Far from pursuing a vain fantasy, we were in fact coming to understand the enormous and satisfying sense of personal wealth that accrues from knowing a place and the reassuring comfort of location that comes from inhabiting it, even if much of that habitation is only imaginative. It was a way of envisioning one possible future at that moment in life when a great many futures are still possible. We were old enough to get some glimpse of the size and shape of those potential territories ahead and to see that some choices would prove more difficult than others, but as yet too young to distinguish which was which, and which in the end the wiser choice. What came out of it, I think, was a recognition that regardless of the specific future, a trout stream would always run through it; that everything wonderful and significant about Jerusalem Creek were things we already owned; that in the ways that matter most, all trout streams are private water.

12

Simple Gifts

~~~~~~~~

I began to see that hope, however feeble its apparent function,

bespeaks allegiance to every unlikely beauty that remains

intact upon Earth.

—David James Duncan, "Birdwatching as a Blood Sport"

Scattered here and there through driftless country, along stream banks and bottomlands, among the rolling hills, tucked back in the crevices of coulees, are farms worked by Amish families who migrated west for all the usual demographic and economic reasons. In a few places, they have settled in numbers large enough to give their community a small but visible public presence—in clusters of farms, in shops selling Amish quilts and furniture and wooden toys. And though three-color chamber of commerce brochures breathlessly invite you to visit "Amish

Country!" these places, so far at least, have failed to produce the kind of embarrassment on display in places like Lancaster County, Pennsylvania, where busloads of tourists lumber in to gawk and point, snapping pictures of chinbeards and buggies as though the whole thing were a spectacle staged for their amusement, failed summer-stock players doing Amish. Amish settlement in the driftless area does not, in fact, date back a great many years, but it is not difficult to see why the place was chosen. In many ways, the terrain and climate recall those of Pennsylvania Dutch country, and the land itself is well scaled to the nonmechanized agricultural practices that have their roots in theological conviction. The farms themselves, and those of the traditional Old Order Amish in particular, are easy to recognize—horse-drawn implements rather than tractors, trucks, and ATVs; no cars in the drive, no power lines or telephone cables running to house and barn. More often than not, they are trim and well maintained, with a clean functionality about them, places of workmanlike character that express one of the central principles of Amish community—the notion of "usefulness," a belief that the work of hands is a thing of moral value.

Among the current generation of agrarian writers and back-to-the-earth types, there has been much interest in the Amish farm as a practical model of sustainable agriculture, as a way of living that strikes environmentally and ethically responsible compromises with the land. Their case has merit: the farms are small in scale; chemical fertilizers and pesticides are kept to a minimum; very little, if any, fossil fuel is used; crop combinations and rotations are chosen to maintain healthy soil; planting and harvesting practices preserve certain types of habitat; and there is a general absence of the wholesale remaking of landscapes that is the hallmark of modern agribusiness. And though I've seen more than one Amish farm where cattle have trampled the banks of a spring creek, and while there are water-quality questions raised by flatland farming methods and manure fertilizers brought to hilly country, I still have no doubt that Amish farms, if perhaps not ideal models, inflict far less damage on the land than the usual alternatives. They present an attractive ecological prospect—so much so, I think, that those who are drawn to it are often persuaded as well by an aesthetic component, a kind of sentimental nostalgia that looks back to, and longs for, a time when the earth was more thoughtfully lived upon and human society less obviously bent on self-destruction, a time in which we enjoyed a closer, more elemental, less exploitative relationship with nature. Even granting that such a time existed, though, there appears to be some confusion about whether the Amish farm is a means of recovering it or merely a romantic emblem of it.

This kind of idealization is common enough. We persist in the wish to see ourselves—if only reflected in the mirror of another culture or another time—as better than we have apparently proven to be. It is a form of spiritual taxidermy often practiced these days on low-technology societies, both past and present; they are stuffed with our desires and plumped up with the values we find missing in our own culture, beginning with a capacity to live harmoniously with the nonhuman environment. And this capacity in turn is attributed to a kind of primitive spiritualism, a respect for the land and reverence for creation grounded in myth or tradition or philosophy or religious teaching that makes any insult to nature not just wrong but unthinkable. Versions of this idea run from the vacuous and creepily New Age to the more restrained but still politically scented interpretations of professional anthropology. And little wonder, since it is an appealing idea, though in the end, I think, an invertebrate one. In my own not cynical, I hope, but more splenetic reading of human affairs, a culture will alter the face of the land in exact proportion to its population and the tools at hand. If a new technology is introduced—horses, or rifles, or chain saws, or snowmobiles—the technologically unsophisticated society will pounce on it for the very rational reason that people living close to the bone have a material interest in making life easier. And because everything lives at the expense of something else, such appropriations always have an environmental cost. History furnishes few examples of a society in which self-restraint has figured to any notable degree.

But there are a few, and Amish society is one of them. Such restraints may issue from some moral feeling for the land, from an interior obligation to respect the intactness of divine creation; it is often presented this way, and it would be nice to think it was the case. It may also be a case of one man doing only as much damage as one man can do, that an Amish farm inflicts itself on the landscape just as far as the boundaries of its technologies will allow; if the population is small and that technology simple, the impact will necessarily be lower. But the most important fact remains: there are voluntary limits. Surrounded by the forces of bigger, faster, and more in a country where the first national impulse—in both nature and culture—is always toward saturation bombing, the Amish farmer chooses methods that leave a lighter footprint on the land. People who look at the Amish farms as agricultural models have a keen interest in determining where the limits are drawn and the consequences to the land that lies within the borders. And no doubt there is much to be learned, or perhaps relearned, from this.

I am more interested in the fact that these limits, these deliberate reductions in scale, exist at all, and in how they are chosen and why maintained. For what is both surprising and heartening is that these farms, and the people for whom they are essential not only as a livelihood but as a fundamental social idea, have managed to endure in a world where the pace and pressure of the new are headspinning even for those who welcome change. Because we see the Amish as very much unlike ourselves—and in fact much of Amish life, the language and style of dress for instance, is designed to underscore just this line between insiders and outsiders—we're apt to attribute their cultural durability to those very differences, to the things that set them apart. They have survived because they have maintained an exclusionary and self-contained society, set and determined in its ways, with strict ideas about the conduct of living. That much is obvious. But there is another component to it, less conspicuous but no less important—not a resistance to new ways but a willingness to entertain them, which in the modern world almost always means confronting technological innovation. Amish life has changed, albeit in ways that we may regard as small, and it has always involved ongoing negotiations both within the community and with the larger world. But the benchmark of negotiating is always the same: what are the merits of change for the community? A great many elements of modern life have been rejected, but often there is compromise. When federal law required dairy farmers to refrigerate the day's milk, the Amish decided to allow electrical cooling equipment to be installed—but the power to run it could not be taken from the grid; to maintain the integrity of the farm, electricity had to be generated on-site or another form of power used. Amish workshops use gas-driven equipment, such as forklifts—but these cannot be used on the farm or for purposes of transportation. Some Amish construct what amount to communal telephone booths, since modern life has made a phone a practical necessity—but a telephone inside the home is prohibited. The Amish do not own cars or even hold driver's licenses; the social status implied by the automobile, particularly in America, is antithetical to their egalitarian principles, and the mobility that a car affords, especially for the young, can threaten the family—keeping them "down on the farm" is not a figure of speech but a real problem in any rural agricultural society. Yet nothing forbids the Amish from accepting rides offered by non-Amish, or even hiring an automobile and driver if circumstances require it.

Such accommodations may seem not only trifling but inconsistent, a form of hairsplitting so fine that it flirts with hypocrisy. The aim, however, is not to draw a line between the inherently good and inherently evil; it is more delicate than that—to distinguish the workable from the unworkable. If you entertain the notion of change by first proposing that the boundaries of community and domestic space have a sacredness about them, then the lines that the Amish have drawn make perfect sense. They do not ask, "Will this change make life easier, or more comfortable, or more profitable?" But, as Wendell Berry says, "The Amish . . . have succeeded simply by asking one question of any proposed innovation, namely: 'What will this do to our community?'" The question is both eminently sane and quite remarkable.

I haven't carried a torch for institutional religion since I was an eleven-year-old altar boy and am not about to start now. But I'm not considering the Amish as a religious organization, although even here I must concede a grudging admiration in some respects—the idea of an Amish TV evangelist, for instance, or an Amish Holy War is so preposterous that it automatically sets the sect apart from most of the world's other denominations. I am far more interested in them as people who have addressed a fundamental human problem: How do you maintain continuity and still move on? How do you hold on to the past and at the same time let it go? The Amish have struck a workable equilibrium between past and present, tradition and technology, nature and culture. They have created their own borders and live in a space that keeps a shared history alive yet one that has made a kind of peace with the present. Such balances involve loss—it is the nature of compromise—and the results are provisional. But to negotiate a settlement with the world, even a tenuous and constantly pressured one, is no mean achievement. The Amish have remained who they are, connected to a communal past that is connected to the land, but have managed as well to survive in an ongoing world. They are, like the landscape itself, driftless, both a memory and a forgetting.

The past is always under siege. There is nothing even distantly resembling wild land left in the driftless area. The history of the upper Midwest, like the history of so many landscapes, is a litany of loss. In 1832, the last bison east of the Mississippi River was killed in Wisconsin. Lumber barons hauled away the vast woods of white pine that once covered northern Wisconsin, Minnesota, and Michigan, and in the course of a single lifetime deforested an area half the size of Europe. Grasslands fell to the plow. The oak savannas and the brook trout are nearly gone. Old-growth forest and virgin prairie exist now only in preserves, a few scattered museum specimens, all small, the total few, just enough to give a glimpse of what once was. They are fascinating places, but it is the fascination of novelty, and the principal effect is to leave you wondering why they are still here at all, what accident of history caused these last few places to be overlooked. The driftless area, like most landscapes on earth, is damaged goods, proof again, were any needed, that we live in a fallen world, and by looks of much of it, fallen from a rather great height. The first loss is always innocence. There is no gainsaying the fact that we have buggered the thing, badly.

But in the quest to preserve what wilderness still remains on earth, it is easy to forget or overlook or, worst of all, dismiss the driftless area and the places like it, the landscapes of home. There is a disturbing voice in modern environmental thinking that regards these tamed lands as already lost, nature's shock troops fallen before human advance, the dead and wounded and missing in action, valuable primarily as grim examples of what must not be allowed to happen elsewhere; they are the potential fate of the real environment that is left. Behind this attitude lies the troubling assumption that the only natural worlds of authentic value, ecologically and spiritually, exist in places untouched and exotic, in the Alaskan wilderness or South American rain forests or Pacific reefs. Nature is out there somewhere, away from us and most emphatically not including us, and indeed this separateness is in part what defines it in the first place. What emerges is a vision in which true nature exists in a few shining islands—refuges, preserves, wilderness areas, places too remote to conquer easily—that rise above the slime pit. Oddly, this vision does not differ to any significant degree, at least in a psychological sense, from the one held by the resource raiders who are responsible for the most egregious abuses. Then again, this similarity may not be so odd after all; it is as easy to factor humans out of the natural equation as it is to factor nature out of the human one. It is, in fact, the same thing. As James Hillman points out, the guardians of the wild wish to do something *for* nature; the despoilers of the wild want to do something *to* or *with* it. But both positions stand apart from the natural world; both are interested in making nature live up to their preconceptions about it. The detachment is the same. You can hear it even in the voices of environmental doom as they condemn our treatment of the land, a certain glee that history is converging on the day when we will at last pay the piper. "Mother Earth will retaliate," writes one of them; "the whole environment will retaliate, and the abuses will be eliminated." This is a morally satisfying prediction, at least compared to the truth. There will be no day of apocalyptic reckoning. Nature does not retaliate; vengeance is a waste of energy and resources. Nature will only adjust, first to us and then, I imagine, without us, and if some of those adjustments hasten our own departure, it's nothing personal, just business, the same one way or another to Mother Earth. Whoever she is.

I am not willing to see domesticated landscapes as chunks of tainted meat thrown to the beast, or to see my love of them—not for their domesticity, or even in spite of it, but along with it—as naïve, misguided, a matter for apology. The life of a landscape, like every life, is a compromise, and you cannot experience a landscape that does not have you in it. Wallace Stegner writes of "deeply lived-in places," and I believe that this is more than just a euphemism for the casualties of war. Driftless country is a deeply lived-in place, and at its worst, the impact of that living has been extremely deep indeed. In some places, the land and water—too tempting, too fertile, too easy to use—have seen rough times. But in the last half century or so, efforts by state agencies, conservation organizations, resident landowners, and fishermen have gone a good distance to halting and, in some places and small ways, even reversing this trend. The evidence is visible in contour farming, public easements, fenced riparian areas, and rotational grazing, in rocks and timbers and in-stream structures—hidden now by decades of vegetative growth—that have stabilized banks and flushed out silt and improved the quality of water. Not all of this has been voluntary or altruistic; great sums of money have changed hands. And while no amount of effort or cash can buy back the past, there are compromises in some places that, for the moment at least, seem workable. They have been aided by the unusual resiliency of these spring-creek landscapes; they are active, fertile, and dynamic, far more so than many other systems. In the high desert of eastern Oregon, wagon tracks cut into the ground by settlers moving west over a century ago are still visible in places, slow-healing scars on a thin, dry soil. In driftless country, the mud ruts of a tractor pressed into the wet April earth are nearly gone by September. We think of agriculture as a conquest of nature, but as any farmer will tell you, it is an ongoing battle against a natural world that continually encroaches and reclaims. The land is always remembering.

There is a possibility of place that lies between the wilds of the upper Amazon and the concrete wasteland of a shopping mall, of land that is used but not used up, domesticated but not enslaved, where valleys and streams have not been forced completely into human disguise. I say this, of course, in part from the perspective of a trout fisherman, which is always myopic, and even as I am fully aware that there is no such thing anymore as a nonpolitical trout. Each one exists by sufferance, by virtue of a land-use restriction, a stream-saving deal, a lawsuit, court injunction, state or federal land designation, a regulation or statute or someone's goodwill. Every fish is one that easily might not have been. To see even these fish as the dominant feature of the landscape may well be valuing them far out of proportion to their actual significance, as occupants of a biological niche or as an indicator species. To regard a place with wild trout as having some measure of environmental integrity may just be another form of self-delusion, but in the end I am a trout fisherman and cannot help but believe that trout express something about the land. There is a narrow line between indifferent resignation to a diminished world and appreciating what gifts still remain.

At one edge of the driftless area, off a bit by itself, lies Lapp's Branch, a lovely spring creek in a very green place. The stream would run through the center of Lapp's Cove were this tiny hamlet big enough to have a center to flow through. It is little more than a short row of houses bounded by a ridge on one side and by the stream on the other. That it has a name at all, I suspect, owes to a need for something to call the baseball team. In this part of the country, having a base-ball team is almost a civic obligation, and considering that almost everyone participates, it doesn't take a town of much size to field nine players. There are local leagues for fast-pitch and slow-pitch, for men and women and children, as well as the informal pickup contests and family rivalries that are settled in the evenings after work or on Saturday morn-ings. Almost every town that has a team also has a field. The diamond at Lapp's Cove is in a pleasant park, not large but well kept. Picnic tables are spread beneath the shade of rows of oaks that flank the first and third baselines. The infield points toward the creek; the distance from home plate to the stream bank is perhaps twenty-five feet, and between them is a high chain-link fence that probably paid for itself long ago in lost baseballs.

The section of Lapp's Branch that meanders up to the edge of the park is pretty fair water. But like all anglers, I pre-fer whenever possible to fish beyond the sight and sound of people, away from barns and buildings and the noise of pass-ing traffic. If I cannot find actual solitude, I will seek out a place on the stream where tall or wooded banks screen out the houses and highways, where I can indulge the illusion of being off alone. Fly fishing is filled with small deceptions of just this sort, about water and fish, flies and techniques. They are little adjustments that the mind works on itself, ways of orchestrating enjoyment to conform with the circumstances at hand. I don't need to know that I'm fishing in the middle of nowhere, but I like it to seem that way as much as possible. So from time to time, if it was the middle of the week and quiet and no one was around, I would spend a few hours fishing the stretch of stream that runs behind the baseball diamond.

On one of these occasions, not so long ago, I found myself on the water when a game was going on, though I wasn't aware of it at first; it must have started after I put in and began wading upstream. As I got closer, I could hear the voices of the people watching the game; the shouts of the players; once in a while, the dull metallic thunk of an aluminum bat meeting a softball; the yelling and laughter of kids horsing around—ordinary sounds that are ordinarily not disagreeable. But when I'm fishing, that level ambient commotion brings out in me a kind of prickliness and irritation that I know even at the time is entirely unjust. I imagine myself imposed upon, that half the reason I came fishing—to enjoy the intimacy of place—is now gone; the other half—catching fish—still remains, but under the circumstances it feels like a lot less than half. The general activity, the noise drifting overhead as I fished, the simple awareness of other people so close by, all were impossible to ignore, and most days I would have packed up my tackle, corralled my various indignations, and retreated to more private water.

But for reasons I cannot explain, I didn't leave and continued working my way upstream until I was just behind home plate. With the high banks and thick vegetation, I couldn't see anything, and was certain that the people in the park had no idea I was there, though a keen eye might have detected the switch of a rod tip back and forth just above the tops of the tall grass. It struck me then that there was a kind of intimacy in this too. It would not have been my first choice of arrangements for fishing, and still would not be, and it by no means produced some gush of expansive sympathy for the universal brotherhood of man. But I was drawn into it in some odd way. We were all in a place we liked, doing something that we enjoyed, staying out of each other's way, observing a kind of compromise unwittingly drawn among strangers in the small space we all occupied. I was fishing on the edge of town. People lived there. The trout were still rising. It wasn't ideal, but it felt strangely like enough.

The terrain of every life, of a landscape or a community or a person, is a series of negotiated settlements, a set of boundaries that always enclose a space of loss. Remembering the past is not the same as returning to it, and moving forward not the same as abandoning it. In negotiating, the question is not how to hold on to or reclaim innocence—that is not possible—but the nature of the bargain struck. It is a prerogative of youth, and one of its great values, to regard compromise as defeat. Later, though, you see it more in the light of a victory, because if you have lived at all, you've seen real defeat, and it looks a good deal different.

13

The Same River Twice

~~~~~~~~~~

The blood still begs direction home.

—Richard Hugo, "The River Now"

The solstice is less than a week away as we travel back to driftless country—Gecko, Lizard and his wife, I and mine—converging from places half a continent away, and a distance in years that feels even greater, to the banks of Mariposa Creek. Our camp is pitched in the shade of a walnut grove, in a setting almost impossibly pastoral—a private valley, skirted on one edge by a road that is not on the way to or from anywhere, and on the other by a quiet little stream that at one time had a reputation for big trout, though I am not sure if this is true any longer. These things come and go, and it doesn't matter to us either way. On a sunny June day, the whole place is alive. Red-tailed hawks coast on thermals rising from the valley. Red-winged blackbirds, those most argumentative of creatures, perch at the tops of trees and shrubs, wings half-extended to show off scarlet shoulder patches, and deliver a raspy trill with such conviction that they quiver all over like a thing about to explode. Butterflies are everywhere—monarchs; red admirals, which will light on the tip of a fly rod held very still; cabbage whites and sulphurs; brilliant speckled fritillaries; and the understated mourning cloaks, which you must see close up to appreciate. The small and gregarious blues puddle together by the dozens on moist soil along the stream to drink in dissolved minerals, and mixed with them in an accidental but stunning composition are enormous yellow tiger swallowtails. So preoccupied are they that you can get close enough to study them through a hand lens, and if disturbed, they erupt into a columnar swirl of confetti wings, a small tornado of colored chips that spirals back down to earth.

Despite rain the day before, the creek runs clear, curling through the meadow, the current carving patterns in the water as varied and shapely as the grain in wood. Spring water spooling through the throat of a pool fans out in the glistening fleck and medullary ripple of quarter-sawn oak. In shallow flats, submerged weeds rumple the surface to a twisted confusion of humps and burls, knots and whirlpools, like a plank of bird's-eye maple. The deep bends are dark with the figured swirls of polished walnut. In calm water near the bank, caddis lumber along the stream bottom, pulling stony cases behind them that plow little trails in the silt. The nymphs of blue-wing olives, the most streamlined of all aquatic insects, built with the fusiform proportions of a tuna, scoot about the *Ranunculus* and elodea, or hold to a leaf with their hind legs, abdomens elevated and wagging from side to side, a curious behavior exhibited by the adult insect as well and for which I have never been able to discover a reason.

Mariposa Creek is not easy water; few spring creeks are. Their difficulty is often attributed to complexity, which gets it, I think, exactly backward. A freestone stream is a more complicated place, its structural variations more numerous for the simple reason that it has a greater repertoire of raw materials from which to fashion them—a wider range of gradients and seasonal water flows working on a mountain's worth of geologic material, from powdery silts to cabin-size blocks of stone. There is an enormous volume of loose matter and ample energy to arrange and rearrange it into a staggering assortment of individual configurations, each its own problem in current and substrate and obstruction. From an architectural point of view, a spring creek is nakedly simple, and that is precisely where the difficulty lies. It does not multiply the variables of moving water but subtracts them. The stream often runs smooth and clear, with no turbulent chutes or drops, and little in the way of riffles or chop. There is no rushing water to mask the sound of your footsteps on the bottom, no swift current to whisk away the surface disturbance of your wading. Nothing about a spring creek hides your presence, or your want of skill, or a faulty presentation, or the inadequacies of tackle or miscalculations of method. It pares away anything that might disguise your mistakes and does away as well with carelessness and incaution in the trout. More than any other type of water, a spring creek makes you appreciate the fact that distortions are an immense advantage to the fisherman; the pure and plain truth is always the hardest to manage.

In the morning and then again in the afternoon, we work upstream, saving the camp water for evening. Most of us rig up with the sentimental favorite, a #16 Deer Hair Caddis, a good opening gambit on many waters but not really a spring-creek pattern, and even less so on a day like today, when nothing remotely caddislike is anywhere to be seen. Bristling with hackle and hair, the fly floats high on the water with an indistinct silhouette, and though a size 16 is not large by most measures, on the silky currents of this narrow creek it looks like a floating toilet brush. But the fly, as I say, is something of a tradition with us and serves at least to keep the fly line strung and in place on the walk upstream, and is easy to replace with something more appropriate when the time comes. As it turns out, we never need to make a change. The fishing is not fast, but trout come steadily throughout the day, where and when you would expect them—on arcing drifts along the outside of a bend, on little exploratory casts made to gaps in the streamside foliage and to indentations along the bank, on ticklish shots to slender channels among the weeds, on more forgiving presentations through chutes or ruffled water or along bubble lines. The fish rise to the fly just often enough so that hope never flags, and just infrequently enough to keep your mind on the fishing, to keep you wondering just where the next trout will come from. You must deliver a short and delicate line, working most spots a few feet at a time, and the tighter ones by inches. The casting is almost nonstop, but with light tackle the cadence is pleasant and not in the least tiring. Perhaps because I came to trout streams in just this way, I find it the most agreeable pace in all of fishing, relaxed and unhurried. You creep forward so as not to disturb the surface, dropping a fly in each promising place, always focused on the water at hand yet always anticipating the next spot, the fresh opportunity ahead. It feels as though you are hardly moving, but on a small stream, you can cover an astonishing amount of water this way.

The fish we catch are all browns, sturdy and well-formed fish, but not large, with one exception—a trout that results from that embarrassing brand of luck that visits every angler from time to time, the preposterous cast that you could not repeat in a lifetime of trying. And the fact of the matter is, I'm not trying at all, but so bungle the cast I'm attempting that it turns into this other thing, completely unplanned and quite inadvertently perfect. The fly drops just millimeters from the bank, at the head of a little tunnel formed by drooping water hemlock, and in an instant is sucked inside by the current. I rip the line off the water, vainly hoping to avert a snag that is all but assured, and, just like that, am tight to a fish. I don't even deserve to feel cheated about not seeing the take. Like most larger trout in these smaller waters this one doesn't run far; there aren't all that many places to go. It clears the water once—a risky tactic in tight quarters, as I've seen more than one fish vault onto dry land—then bores head-down into the weeds and hugs the bottom a while before I manage at last to get a hand around it.

It is a fine-looking and girthy trout, nearly nineteen inches long, the biggest I have ever landed in these spring creeks. One should be grateful, I suppose, for good fortune, but I think most fly fishermen will understand my disappointment in the episode. A fish like this doesn't count. I meant to catch it, but didn't catch it the way I meant to—a distinction that nonanglers often find idiotic, the way in which the whole matter hinges at least as much on our intentions as on the results. Luck and happenstance are always a part of fishing, though for the most part, I think, in small and subtle ways that an angler never notices. But the aim of fishing is to fish well, and the aim of fishing well is to make chance count for as little as possible. Much of the pleasure comes from knowing, or at least preserving the illusion, that we are the agents of our own success, that we have orchestrated the whole affair ourselves, that a trout is not hooked through some quirky turn of events, but that it willingly and predictably responds to our own ideas about how it ought to behave. The accidental trout fails to satisfy because it is an unrepeatable phenomenon; it means nothing but that accidents happen. So, as I say, a fish of this sort doesn't count; it has, at best, a sort of fluky entertainment value, like a tee shot that caroms off the clubhouse for a hole in one.

Lizard, to whom I relate the tale a short time afterward, is unsympathetic. "Figures." He shrugs. "You're not that good."

The fishing tapers off after dinner, though we have staked our fortunes on shaky ground, sitting on the bank at dusk waiting for the hatch of giant *Hexagenia* mayflies, a local and unpredictable event but spectacular when it comes off. Unlike most mayfly species, the hexes don't live among the rocks or weeds or detritus of the bottom; they tunnel into the streambed or banks, digging a U-shaped burrow with two openings. But not all substrates lend themselves to this kind of construction. A firmly compacted or rocky bottom is too resistant to excavate; a tunnel dug in overly soft material, like a loose slurry of silt, will collapse. The nymphs prefer to dig in banks and streambeds composed of a particularly gummy, stiff muck. Many spring creeks have little or none of it, and even those with a reputation for good hex populations, Lapp's Branch, for instance, have it only in places, which can make the hatch spotty and irregular. One fisherman might be mopping up while another, a hundred yards away, is getting only mosquito bites. Anglers who have dialed into the right places stay pretty close-mouthed about them—at least no one's told me—and I might as well come clean right now, forfeit whatever credibility I have, and admit that I've never once caught a hex hatch on any of the spring creeks in driftless country. I might plead extenuating circumstances—for one, I don't care much about fishing after dark, when the mayflies emerge—but the fact is, I've given it a fair shot and have never managed to hit it right. And considering the bushwhacking with a flashlight held in your teeth, slogging through the mud in the dark, and staring into the pitch black swatting mosquitoes, I concluded some time back that I'm much better off at camp drinking a beer. Doubtless I'd feel differently about it had the bugs done their part.

I have seen hexes on the glacial lakes farther north and, on a few occasions, hatches that beggar description, including one evening as I was sitting at the end of a dock on a sheltered little inlet, rimmed with pines. I know from dropping and raising a rowboat anchor thousands of times that the bay is about twelve feet deep and the bottom a mixture of mud and sand. It must be ideal habitat, for just before sunset, the flies started popping—little surface disturbances that I took at first to be small fish until each ripple produced the unmistakable profile of a floating mayfly, silhouetted against the glassy water. Their wings dried slowly in the cool, damp air, and the first flies rested on the water for many minutes; in the meantime, more and more of them kept coming until the bay was strewn with acres of hex duns. There was surprisingly little surface feeding for a lake filled with panfish and smallmouth, though I imagine the real carnage was taking place underwater, in that long, twelve-foot wriggle to the top. I was there a week, and this happened just once. On the other six evenings, to all appearances identical, not a single fly showed up, and as we watch a quiet pool on Mariposa Creek in the gathering darkness, it turns out to be another one of those nights.

Every trip finds its own tempo, and this one is brisk, with a dozen trout streams nearby, only a few days to fish, and a lot of lost time to make up for. After breakfast each morning, we strike out in a different direction to different streams, most of them new to me. We have better maps now and Lizard to assume the duties of guide. While my brother and I left the Midwest some time back, Lizard and his wife have remained behind and learned new waters and come to feel at home in driftless country, not yet aware that in a few short years they too will head west. We fish a few familiar places and spend time scouting others, stopping at bridges to size up the water, maybe giving it a whirl for an hour just to see what turns up or staying half a day if things pan out. But sooner or later we move on to another spot, and then another, and when evening falls head back to camp for a late dinner, too bushed to wait for the hexes. Almost every creek gives up a few trout, though on Agate Fork, where rumor has it that a small population of native brook trout still holds on, we catch nothing at all. But it is a hot and bright afternoon, so we don't jump to any conclusions.

Near the end of the week, Lizard and his wife must pull up stakes—duty calls—and though they go at it with dawdling reluctance, their gear is at last packed up. We resolve to repeat the trip, not to wait so long the next time, and gamely venture a few tentative possibilities even as we know that the reunion of the last few days owed much to luck and that returning to this place grows less probable with each passing year. They are old friends and good ones, and I find myself missing them before they are even gone. And then all at once they are. There are times when the greater part of life seems a leave-taking.

My wife and brother and I are not due back for a couple of days, but we too break camp; though not ready to call it quits yet, it's better to move on than to hang around, the last desperate revelers trying in vain to prolong a party that is already over. We decide to take our time, fishing our way back to the town where my brother and I grew up, before leaving for home in the West. There is no particular plan; Gecko has the wheel and I am content to let him follow his own whims in the matter. We stop at a few places here and there to look at the water, but never uncase our rods and continue on, tacking a course south and east along winding county black-tops that carry us back to a part of spring-creek country that we know well. Coming to a familiar crossroads, Gecko slows and turns right, onto a road that could only be taking us to Emerald Creek. Half an hour later, in a light drizzle, he pulls over at a small bridge where you might stand and look up-stream at clear water whispering over a channel soft with the weave of a hundred greens, like the pile of a Persian rug.

My brother cuts cross-country to a stretch of water above us; my wife and I put in at the bridge and share a rod. The overcast sky and misty rain make perfect weather for a blue-wing olive hatch, but not a single fly appears. We work up a hundred yards or so, taking a trout or two, when all at once, we are into fish. There's not a rise in sight, but the trout are everywhere, in the best spots and in the unlikely places, rav-enous little wild browns. Spring-creek trout have a reputa-tion for being moody, which most often means they are difficult, but when they're in the mood to feast, almost noth-ing—not sloppy wading, not poor casting, not a ridiculous choice of flies—will dissuade them. It is difficult to say much about these times other than that, once in a very great while, they happen, and they have nothing whatsoever to do with you. It's like a hatch with no bugs, and fishing that is ordinar-ily tough, often to the point of futility, suddenly turns easier than a rugby match against the Little Sisters of the Poor.

We take nothing large at all, despite several fly changes calculated to that end, but for well over an hour hook eight-inch trout on every second or third cast. It is remarkable how this kind of fishing, fast and effortless, can so rapidly lose its charm. We labor to this very purpose, and when a rare mo-ment delivers the thing we have hoped for, our interest fades. It is another of the fisherman's peculiarities that bewilder the nonangler, and I am sometimes puzzled myself and left won-dering just what we want out of all of this. When the beauty of place and the pleasure of our surroundings and the company of friends are stripped away and all that remains is the catching of fish, how narrow becomes the band of circumstances that really satisfy. On the other hand, Emerald Creek has had its way with me more times than I can remember, and I'm not giving up right away no matter how easy the fishing is. You seize those occasions that look like justice because you never know whether another one will come along.

When we meet up with my brother later, he too, it turns out, has had good fishing. He snips the fly from the leader and reels up the line. "Comrades," he says, "I believe our work here is done." The rain has stopped, leaving the air thick with moisture. He holds out the keys to me, but I shake my head. We climb into the car and sit for a minute as it idles, waiting for the windows to clear. At last he pulls around, backtracking the route we took in, and at the first turn swings northwest, on the road that leads to Jerusalem Creek, which I am certain now is where we had been headed from the beginning.

I haven't seen the stream in several years, and as we descend into the coulee and drive along the bank, I am surprised not by the place but by the cliché of my own reaction. Everything—the creek, the valley, the bordering ridges; the stretch of water and piece of land we once imagined owning—all look smaller than I remember. I suppose I have pictured them in memory as we often do the places and people we love, with the first pair of eyes through which we saw them rather than the last. Such an image may not be accurate, but it is in some ways more faithful.

Old places, even those you once knew intimately and still remember well, sometimes possess a surprising weight when you return to them. The physical circumstances have a way of making you relive the life of the person you were back when the place was familiar. You do not so much recollect old thoughts, you rethink them; you don't recall feelings you had, but feel them again. You are drawn to inhabit the place as you once did, but this time with the inescapable duality of watching yourself be the person you were before, of experiencing yourself experiencing life as you once did. The most commonplace details trigger an explosion of old associations, and you linger over them as you would the effects of a departed friend, studying an empty pair of boots worn into the shape of feet or a silent guitar that still suggests the hands that played it. You believe yourself to be summoning former times, but that is untrue. The weight that you feel exists in the present, not in the past. You can call it nostalgia or sentimentality, but it is really a kind of mourning, and you are the one who has died. The person you were then no longer exists.

A fisherman's first trout stream is a kind of first love that has much in common with first loves of other sorts. It is deeply and sometimes comically uninformed by experience, graceless and improvisational, felt with a passion often beyond its merit. And first loves are seldom the best ones, much as we may think otherwise at the time. They are too, by definition, one-of-a-kind, unique. There is a first time for everything, but only one first for each, and that time carries with it an irreproducible freshness that may be the most enduring part of it all. Perceptions, impressions, and details may erode from memory and leave in their place only the luminous and intense newness with which they were once felt. First loves also teach, but whether or not you learn anything is another matter. I realized long ago that Jerusalem Creek was at best a second-rate trout stream, though I didn't know this when I began fishing there, nor would I have cared even if I could have been made to believe it. There were trout in its waters, and in my eyes, that made it magnificent. It still does, but there is a sadness about it too now, as there is with all the places and times that have briefly concentrated within their small borders something like the whole of life. Things disappear, and what remains is tinged with some unlocated longing, the pinch of a fugitive loneliness.

I cannot fish this feeling away, set it adrift on the current to let it dissolve in something larger than itself. For fly fishing is a thing of no particular intrinsic worth; it is arbitrary and trivial, valueless beyond one's love of it, though this can be said about a great many things and even a few important ones. A trout stream might be therapeutic at times, but it is not finally a form of therapy, not a trip to the shrink or a heart-to-heart with the preacher or a little treat from the pharmacy. In the odd and unbidden moment, it may surrender some insight, but if you fish for enlightenment, you better be sure first that you can stand the glare.

Under an overcast sky, on a warm and windless and deep-green afternoon, we walk the banks of Jerusalem Creek for a while with no intention of fishing. It is not quite beating the bounds, though something like it, but much time has passed and much is unfamiliar. Instead, we retrace the old meanders, now the cutoff oxbows and abandoned channels where years ago a stream once flowed. My wife listens patiently to the stories.

In early evening, we drive a few miles upstream and pitch a tent on the upper end of the stream where it is too small and shallow for trout. Not far from here, the first small beginnings of the creek rise from a spring hidden in the tangled undergrowth on the flank of a hill. It flows past where we are camped, through a low corridor of green, and you might overlook it altogether were it not for the sound of water washing over a bed of worn limestone broken from the hills. It is the longest day of the year, but night comes early beneath the clouded sky. No stars appear, and when the last light vanishes, we turn in.

There is a strange effect produced by the sound of trickling water, not the rush and surge of a big river or the cascading of a small stream in the mountains but the soft purling of a tiny brook through the stones. You notice it most at night in a tent just a few feet away, as you enter that unguarded and twilit territory just this side of sleep. If it is quiet, the trickle begins to sound like voices, not one or two but dozens, modulated and reverberating like the rise and fall of conversation in a crowded room. The talk, though not loud, is animated and lively; everyone is speaking at once. You cannot pick out a single voice, tease it away from the ripples and rolls of the background. But now and then, a small group of voices lifts briefly above the others, swelling for a moment in what sounds like laughter, as though someone's made an amusing remark, then dissolves again into the collective undercurrent. It is a most convincing illusion, and at times, persuaded that people have gathered outside, I have summoned myself almost fully awake before realizing that no one was there, that it was only the stream. This sound is not the voice of the water talking to you. It is, in a way, not even sound at all. It is the mind's restless inclination to find order in the unpatterned, to search for meaning in randomness, to resolve the unfamiliar into the familiar. So insistent is this propensity that we will not abandon it even when it deceives, so deeply rooted that it is the last thing we surrender before drifting into the unconsciousness of sleep—and perhaps not even then. Like the pumping of blood, this seeking of sense from the senseless may continue beyond our awareness to become the strange heart that gives life to our dreaming. It is the reason too that all rivers run backward to the first one, and all writing about them ends up as memory.

Afterword
A Workable Deception

~~~~~~~~~~

The language of fly fishing is essentially a language of imitation. We speak of "naturals" and their "representation," use the word "wings" to refer equally to the appendages on a mayfly and those on a dry-fly hook, and interchangeably call both the creature and our creation a "blue-wing olive." We tie a fly to "simulate" an insect, fish it in a "lifelike" manner, and in general do all we can to make it look and act "real." That the words of fly fishing surround the idea of faithful representation comes as no surprise to the fly tyer and fisherman; it is the most delicate and exacting of tasks, and in the end, of course, an impossible one. We cannot duplicate, only approximate, and even then in the crudest of terms. But preoccupied as it is with imitation, the language misleads, for imitation is not the principal end of fly fishing, only a means. The goal itself is deception, the perpetration of a lie, and the more you consider that the trout is not the only creature deceived, the closer this idea comes to the heart of fly fishing. When we catch a trout, we flatter ourselves not merely that we have fooled a fish but that our deception represents a kind of understanding about it. This supposition, however, is by no means certain, and much of the time, I think, the case is precisely opposite—our understanding represents a kind of deception.

Take for a moment that category of nonspecific, all-purpose artificial flies that we call "attractor patterns" because they imitate nothing in particular. The Woolly Bugger is a good example—a simple but remarkable pattern in moving or still waters, fished dead-drift or on the swing, stripped or twitched. Anglers will account for its effectiveness by explaining that a trout "took it for," depending on the circumstances, a stonefly nymph, a sculpin, a crayfish, a hellgrammite, a leech, a minnow, a dragonfly nymph, or something else. I have said these same things myself. But the similarity between a Woolly Bugger and these various and quite different aquatic creatures taxes even a fisherman's credulity, and unlike the trout, we don't make these distinctions for a living. We don't really know—not really—what caused a trout to take the fly, and it is entirely possible that the fish didn't take it "for" anything in particular or, for that matter, even anything edible. Clearly, somewhere a reason exists, yet we cannot know it because we cannot know what goes on inside the head of a trout. But we invent little fictions anyway because we need an explanation; it is not enough to catch the fish—we must know why.

Attractor patterns may appear to be a special case, an extreme instance, but I don't think it is at all exceptional. Take a more classic, if less common, situation: a pod of trout in a slow, smooth pool, rising to a hatch of pale morning duns. You choose your best fly, lay it out on your best drag-free float, and catch a fish. The conclusion, that you deceived the trout into believing that your fly was a real pale morning dun, seems self-evident—but only if you choose to believe that the trout was unable to detect the counterfeit, to distinguish the imitation from a living insect. And no fisherman of any real experience would put much stock in that idea. A trout is a primitive creature, but it is exceedingly well made and possesses superb vision. Fishing lakes in early spring, I've caught trout gorged to the gills with daphnia, tiny crustaceans smaller than a wind knot in 7X tippet. The resolving power of a trout's eye is more than equal to perceiving the smallest signs of fraud in a trout fly and so must be keenly aware of the larger ones—a steel ring projecting from one end of the body, for instance, and a steel hook from the other. And while we may present such a fly with the greatest imaginable skill, there is finally no such thing as a "drag-free float." No matter how long or light the leader, how perfect the cast, our imitation can never replicate the exquisite independence of a mayfly on the water, resting on six tiny saucers pressed into the surface film, drifting without even getting its feet wet. A fish that does not see these differences must quite literally be blind.

If we admit that a trout can see all those things that betray an artificial fly—hook and leader and drag, certainly, but smaller details too—then we are left to draw one of two conclusions. First, the trout sees but does not "care." For some reason, it dismisses these unnatural anomalies and takes the fly; it looks good enough. This, I think, is what we hope for and what most fishermen believe occurs, though it gets us no closer to any useful accounting for the trout's indifference to the signs of deception, particularly since it sometimes happens and sometimes doesn't. Yet it is just as possible that the trout notices the imperfections in an artificial fly and does care, that those very features that make the counterfeit unlike the natural fly are in fact responsible for its appeal. I once fished the Trico spinner fall on Silver Creek, tried pattern after pattern and was roundly humiliated, until I tied on a #16 Royal Wulff—a reliable fly under many circumstances, but drifting among thousands of tiny delicate mayflies, a pattern about as subtle as a drive-by shooting. But it worked, as I'm sure a similar tactic has worked for other anglers, since this do-something-different approach is a minor chestnut of fly-fishing wisdom. And in fact, I strongly suspect that the type of specialty flies that are hilarious to nonfishermen but popular with the evangelical hatch-matchers—stillborn duns, crippled emergers, crumpled spinners—succeed not because they imitate these unfortunates but because they look different from anything else on the water. Of course, this is only my explanation, and plenty of evidence supports exactly the opposite conclusion—and that is the point. We think we know, yet the fact that anglers hold not just widely different opinions on the subject but completely contradictory ones and that all explanations end up working about equally well suggests that we have gone no great distance in establishing anything.

We may, in very local circumstances, deceive the trout often enough to persuade ourselves that we understand why they do what they do, but such solutions do not travel well. The next day or the next river gives them the lie. Our explanations work just often enough to keep us believing and fail just often enough to make us suspicious that they are only smoke. We cannot, in the end, tell if a particular trout takes or rejects an artificial fly because it looks like a natural one, or because it doesn't, or for some other reason. Much is known about the trout's optical system, but nothing at all about how a visual image registers in its brain; we know how a trout sees, but not what it sees. And we will almost surely never know.

Such uncertainty is profoundly unsatisfying because it reduces fishing to the arbitrary, random, and accidental—which, at times, it very much seems to be. So we begin with the assumption, because we really have no choice, that every trout does what it does for a reason, and though it is the logic of instinct rather than rationality, it is a logic nonetheless. The trout does not behave from capriciousness or perversity or whim; these, paradoxically, appear to be functions of a bigger brain. Whether a fish accepts or refuses a fly, it has made a certain sense of it in either case, and we in turn are compelled to make it make sense to ourselves, to begin with the premise that the world operates according to discoverable principles. So we collect what we have observed and surmised and experienced in the past and gather these together in a fragile skein of disputable inferences, a wispy web of causes and effects that attempt to explain the inexplicable. And the task of mind, like that of the fly tyer's craft, is not to reproduce real life, because that is not possible, but to create a convincing fabrication, a workable fiction.

In the end it is all about stories. A trout fly is only a story we invent, a tale spun on a hook shank from the imperfect materials at hand, ordered according to our best guess, an explanation of what we think we understand about a world. Casting it on the water, we tell our story to the trout and look for signs. Sometimes it convinces, sometimes it does not. But either way, we invent another story, this time to tell ourselves, about why things should have happened the way that they did. And when our stories fail, as all eventually do, we sift our failures for clues and give them names and out of the names make up a new story, hoping to converge on some truth of the matter even as we know that is impossible, and settling as we must for the best of all possible lies.

This thing of causes and effects will not leave us alone; it lodges like a burr in the brain. We are the sum of all we remember, a calculus of our own explanations, always revising the tangible artifacts of memory into the person we are now, devising the stories that map the landscape of the life we've lived. Some stories are told through a gradual accretion, the way a pearl is a tale told by an oyster about a certain grain of sand. Some are told by a wearing away, a slow erosion through strata to expose the fragments of the past. And some stories are driftless and told both ways. It is always a fitting together, layer upon layer, memory against memory, but never enough to make the story whole. There are always the gaps of things forgotten or missing or lost, gaps so great sometimes that what remains serves only to define the edges of the empty space it surrounds. And this may be the truest way to tell a story about a thing that isn't there.

But the story isn't quite true, because the pieces never fit exactly, and so we knap the edges and grind down the rough spots and polish the surfaces of some and join them with others already tumbled smooth with remembering, only to discover in these reworkings that the pieces now go together in a dozen different ways, each as adaptable to the needs of the tale as the tale to the needs of the teller. There is no blueprint. Every story is provisional and contingent, a compromise of sorts, less true for what it is than for what it seems. And all that is said about landscapes and water, the intimacy of scale, about memory and names and loss—are all inventions, stories told in the trust that at bottom some secret heart exists, because that is the only thing that would make our stories matter. We believe in them even as we know them for fabrications, for an ignorance so well-ordered that it

simulates knowledge. Our stories may convince only ourselves, but that is why we make them, to build something
sturdy enough to bear the weight of explanation, smooth
enough to ease a passage through the world.

But there is a final irony, a lingering possibility that the
fiction you turned out in the hope it was workable turned out
to be exactly right. Through insight or accident, all the pieces
fit, and your story arrived at the bottom of things, and you
couldn't even tell. Because there is no way of knowing.

In the end, perhaps, all that remains is a trust that the
small spaces we fish in our minds are real; that currents will
mirror the streambed and surfaces answer to depths; that
spring water carries the pulse of its source, and that the trout
that swim there, if they could speak, might explain how
things come to pass.